Harvard
Business
Review

ON

MANAGING PROJECTS

THE HARVARD BUSINESS REVIEW PAPERBACK SERIES

The series is designed to bring today's managers and professionals the fundamental information they need to stay competitive in a fast-moving world. From the preeminent thinkers whose work has defined an entire field to the rising stars who will redefine the way we think about business, here are the leading minds and landmark ideas that have established the *Harvard Business Review* as required reading for ambitious businesspeople in organizations around the globe.

Other books in the series:

Harvard Business Review Interviews with CEOs

Harvard Business Review on Advances in Strategy

Harvard Business Review on Appraising Employee Performance

Harvard Business Review on Becoming a High Performance Manager

Harvard Business Review on Brand Management

Harvard Business Review on Breakthrough Leadership

Harvard Business Review on Breakthrough Thinking

Harvard Business Review on Building Personal and Organizational Resilience

Harvard Business Review on Business and the Environment

Harvard Business Review on the Business Value of IT

Harvard Business Review on Change

Harvard Business Review on Compensation

Harvard Business Review on Corporate Ethics

Harvard Business Review on Corporate Governance

Harvard Business Review on Corporate Responsibility

Harvard Business Review on Corporate Strategy

Harvard Business Review on Crisis Management

Harvard Business Review on Culture and Change

Harvard Business Review on Customer Relationship Management

Harvard Business Review

ON

MANAGING PROJECTS

The *Harvard Business Review* articles in this collection are available as individual reprints. Discounts apply to quantity purchases. For information and ordering, please contact Customer Service, Harvard Business School Publishing, Boston, MA 02163. Telephone: (617) 783-7500 or (800) 988-0886, 8 A.M. to 6 P.M. Eastern Time, Monday through Friday. Fax: (617) 783-7555, 24 hours a day. E-mail: custserv@hbsp.harvard.edu.

Library of Congress Cataloging-in-Publication Data
Harvard business review on managing projects.
    p.   cm. — (The Harvard business review paperback series)
    Includes index.
    ISBN 1-59139-639-5
    1. Project management. I. Harvard Business School. II. Harvard business review. III. Series.
HD69.P75H374 2005
658.4´04—dc22   2004016504
                                         CIP

The paper used in this publication meets the minimum requirements of the American National Standard for Information Sciences—Permanence of Paper for Printed Library Materials, ANSI Z39.48–1992.

Contents

Harvard Business Review

ON

MANAGING PROJECTS

Why Good Projects Fail Anyway

NADIM F. MATTA AND

RONALD N. ASHKENAS

Executive Summary

BIG PROJECTS FAIL AT an astonishing rate—more than half the time, by some estimates. It's not hard to understand why. Complicated long-term projects are customarily developed by a series of teams working along parallel tracks. If managers fail to anticipate everything that might fall through the cracks, those tracks will not converge successfully at the end to reach the goal.

Take a companywide CRM project. Traditionally, one team might analyze customers, another select the software, a third develop training programs, and so forth. When the project's finally complete, though, it may turn out that the salespeople won't enter in the requisite data because they don't understand why they need to. This very problem has, in fact, derailed many CRM programs at major organizations.

1

There is a way to uncover unanticipated problems while the project is still in development. The key is to inject into the overall plan a series of miniprojects, or "rapid-results initiatives," which each have as their goal a miniature version of the overall goal. In the CRM project, a single team might be charged with increasing the revenues of one sales group in one region by 25% within four months. To reach that goal, team members would have to draw on the work of all the parallel teams. But in just four months, they would discover the salespeople's resistance and probably other unforeseen issues, such as, perhaps, the need to divvy up commissions for joint-selling efforts.

The World Bank has used rapid-results initiatives to great effect to keep a sweeping 16-year project on track and deliver visible results years ahead of schedule. In taking an in-depth look at this project, and others, the authors show why this approach is so effective and how the initiatives are managed in conjunction with more traditional project activities.

Big PROJECTS FAIL AT an astonishing rate. Whether major technology installations, postmerger integrations, or new growth strategies, these efforts consume tremendous resources over months or even years. Yet as study after study has shown, they frequently deliver disappointing returns—by some estimates, in fact, well over half the time. And the toll they take is not just financial. These failures demoralize employees who have labored diligently to complete their share of the work. One middle manager at a top pharmaceutical company told us,

"I've been on dozens of task teams in my career, and I've never actually seen one that produced a result."

The problem is, the traditional approach to project management shifts the project teams' focus away from the end result toward developing recommendations, new technologies, and partial solutions. The intent, of course, is to piece these together into a blueprint that will achieve the ultimate goal, but when a project involves many people working over an extended period of time, it's very hard for managers planning it to predict all the activities and work streams that will be needed. Unless the end product is very well understood, as it is in highly technical engineering projects such as building an airplane, it's almost inevitable that some things will be left off the plan. And even if all the right activities have been anticipated, they may turn out to be difficult, or even impossible, to knit together once they're completed.

Managers use project plans, timelines, and budgets to reduce what we call "execution risk"—the risk that designated activities won't be carried out properly—but they inevitably neglect these two other critical risks—the "white space risk" that some required activities won't be identified in advance, leaving gaps in the project plan, and the "integration risk" that the disparate activities won't come together at the end. So project teams can execute their tasks flawlessly, on time and under budget, and yet the overall project may still fail to deliver the intended results.

We've worked with hundreds of teams over the past 20 years, and we've found that by designing complex projects differently, managers can reduce the likelihood that critical activities will be left off the plan and increase the odds that all the pieces can be properly integrated at the end. The key is to inject into the overall plan a series of miniprojects—what we call *rapid-results initiatives*—each staffed with a team responsible for a version of the hoped-for overall result in miniature and each designed to deliver its result quickly.

Let's see what difference that would make. Say, for example, your goal is to double sales revenue over two years by implementing a customer relationship management (CRM) system for your sales force. Using a traditional project management approach, you might have one team research and install software packages, another analyze the different ways that the company interacts with customers (e-mail, telephone, and in person, for example), another develop training programs, and so forth. Many months later, however, when you start to roll out the program, you might discover that the salespeople aren't sold on the benefits. So even though they may know how to enter the requisite data into the system, they refuse. This very problem has, in fact, derailed many CRM programs at major organizations.

But consider the way the process might unfold if the project included some rapid-results initiatives. A single team might take responsibility for helping a small number of users—say, one sales group in one region— increase their revenues by 25% within four months. Team members would probably draw on all the activities described above, but to succeed at their goal, the microcosm of the overall goal, they would be forced to find out what, if anything, is missing from their plans as they go forward. Along the way, they would, for example, discover the salespeople's resistance, and they would be compelled to educate the sales staff about the system's benefits. The team may also discover that it needs to tackle other issues, such as how to divvy up commissions on sales resulting from cross-selling or joint-selling efforts.

When they've ironed out all the kinks on a small scale, their work would then become a model for the next teams, which would either engage in further rapid-results initiatives or roll the system out to the whole organization—but now with a higher level of confidence that the project will have the intended impact on sales revenue. The company would see an early payback on its investment and gain new insights from the team's work, and the team would have the satisfaction of delivering real value.

In the pages that follow, we'll take a close look at rapid-results initiatives, using case studies to show how these projects are selected and designed and how they are managed in conjunction with more traditional project activities.

How Rapid-Results Teams Work

Let's look at an extremely complex project, a World Bank initiative begun in June 2000 that aims to improve the productivity of 120,000 small-scale farmers in Nicaragua by 30% in 16 years. A project of this magnitude entails many teams working over a long period of time, and it crosses functional and organizational boundaries.

They started as they had always done: A team of World Bank experts and their clients in the country (in this case, Ministry of Agriculture officials) spent many months in preparation—conducting surveys, analyzing data, talking to people with comparable experiences in other countries, and so on. Based on their findings, these project strategists, designers, and planners made an educated guess about the major streams of work that would be required to reach the goal. These work streams included reorganizing government institutions that give technical advice to farmers, encouraging the creation of a private-sector market in agricultural support services (such as helping farmers adopt new farming technologies and use improved seeds), strengthening the National Institute for Agricultural Technology (INTA), and establishing an information management system that would help agricultural R&D institutions direct their efforts to the most productive areas of research. The result of all this preparation was a multiyear project plan, a document laying out the work streams in detail.

But if the World Bank had kept proceeding in the traditional way on a project of this magnitude, it would have been years before managers found out if something had been left off the plan or if the various work streams could be integrated—and thus if the project would ultimately achieve its goals. By that time, millions of dollars would have been invested and much time potentially wasted. What's more, even if everything worked according to plan, the project's beneficiaries would have been waiting for years before seeing any payoff from the effort. As it happened, the project activities proceeded on schedule, but a new minister of agriculture came on board two years in and argued that he needed to see results sooner than the plan allowed. His complaint resonated with Norman Piccioni, the World Bank team leader, who was also getting impatient with the project's pace. As he said at the time, "Apart from the minister, the farmers, and me, I'm not sure anyone working on this project is losing sleep over whether farmer productivity will be improved or not."

Over the next few months, we worked with Piccioni to help him and his clients add rapid-results initiatives to the implementation process. They launched five teams, which included not only representatives from the existing work streams but also the beneficiaries of the project, the farmers themselves. The teams differed from traditional implementation teams in three fundamental ways. Rather than being partial, horizontal, and long term, they were results oriented, vertical, and fast. A look at each attribute in turn shows why they were more effective.

RESULTS ORIENTED

As the name suggests, a rapid-results initiative is intentionally commissioned to produce a measurable result, rather than recommendations, analyses, or partial solutions. And even though the goal is on a smaller scale than the overall objective, it is nonetheless challenging. In Nicaragua, one team's goal was to increase Grade A milk production in the Leon municipality from 600 to 1,600 gallons per day in 120 days in 60 small and medium-size producers. Another was to increase pig weight on 30 farms by 30% in 100 days using enhanced corn seed. A third was to secure commitments from private-sector experts to provide technical advice and agricultural support to 150 small-scale farmers in the El Sauce (the dry farming region) within 100 days.

This results orientation is important for three reasons. First, it allows project planners to test whether the activities in the overall plan will add up to the intended result and to alter the plans if need be. Second, it produces real benefits in the short term. Increasing pig weight in 30 farms by 30% in just over three months is useful to those 30 farmers no matter what else happens in the project. And finally, being able to deliver results is more rewarding and energizing for teams than plodding along through partial solutions.

The focus on results also distinguishes rapid-results initiatives from pilot projects, which are used in traditionally managed initiatives only to reduce execution risk. Pilots typically are designed to test a preconceived solution, or means, such as a CRM system, and to work out implementation details before rollout. Rapid-results initiatives, by contrast, are aimed squarely at reducing white space and integration risk.

VERTICAL

Project plans typically unfold as a series of activities represented on a timeline by horizontal bars. In this context, rapid-results initiatives are vertical. They encompass a slice of several horizontal activities, implemented in tandem in a very short time frame. By using the term "vertical," we also suggest a cross-functional effort, since different horizontal work streams usually include people from different parts of an organization (or even, as in Nicaragua, different organizations), and the vertical slice brings these people together. This vertical orientation is key to reducing white space and integration risks in the overall effort: Only by uncovering and properly integrating any activities falling in the white space between the horizontal project streams will the team be able to deliver its miniresult. (For a look at the horizontal and vertical work streams in the Nicaragua project, see the exhibit "The World Bank's Project Plan.")

The team working on securing commitments between farmers and technical experts in the dry farming region, for example, had to knit together a broad set of activities. The experts needed to be trained to deliver particular services that the farmers were demanding because they had heard about new ways to increase their productivity through the information management system. That, in turn, was being fed information coming out of INTA's R&D efforts, which were directed toward addressing specific problems the farmers had articulated. So team members had to draw on a number of the broad horizontal activities laid out in the overall project plan and integrate them into their vertical effort. As they did so, they discovered that they had to add activities missing from the original horizontal work streams. Despite the team members' heroic efforts to integrate the ongoing activities, for instance, 80 days into their 100-day initiative, they had secured only half the commitments they were aiming for. Undeterred and spurred on by the desire to accomplish their goal, team members drove through the towns of the region announcing with loudspeakers the availability and benefits of the technical services. Over the following 20 days, the gap to the goal was closed. To close the white space in the project plan, "marketing of technical services" was added as another horizontal stream.

FAST

How fast is fast? Rapid-results projects generally last no longer than 100 days. But they are by no means quick fixes, which imply shoddy or short-term solutions. And while they deliver quick wins, the more important value of these initiatives is that they change the way teams approach their work. The short time frame fosters a sense of personal challenge, ensuring that team members feel a sense of urgency right from the start that leaves no time to squander on big studies or interorganizational bickering. In traditional horizontal work streams, the

The World Bank's Project Plan

A project plan typically represents the planned activities as horizontal bars plotted over time. But in most cases, it's very difficult to accurately assess all the activities that will be required to complete a complicated long-term project. We don't know what will fall into the white space between the bars. It's also difficult to know whether these activities can be integrated seamlessly at the end; the teams working in isolation may develop solutions that won't fit together. Rapid-results initiatives cut across horizontal activities, focusing on a miniversion of the overall result rather than on a set of activities.

Here is a simplified version of the Nicaragua project described in this article. Each vertical team (depicted as a group by the vertical bar) includes representatives from every horizontal team, which makes the two types of initiatives mutually reinforcing. So, for example, the horizontal work stream labeled "Set up private-sector market in agricultural support services" includes activities like developing a system of coupons to subsidize farmers' purchases. The vertical team establishing service contracts between technical experts and farmers drew on this work, providing the farmers with coupons they could use to buy the technical services. This, in turn, drove competition in the private sector, calling on the work that the people on the horizontal training teams were doing—which led to better services.

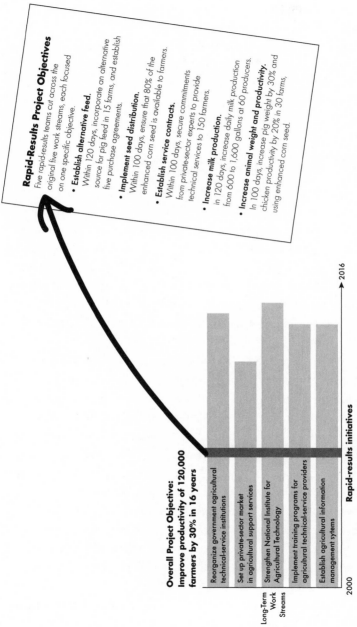

gap between current status and the goal starts out far wider, and a feeling of urgency does not build up until a short time before the day of reckoning. Yet it is precisely at that point that committed teams kick into a high-creativity mode and begin to experiment with new ideas to get results. That kick comes right away in rapid-results initiatives.

A Shift in Accountability

In most complex projects, the executives shaping and assigning major work streams assume the vast majority of the responsibility for the project's success. They delegate execution risk to project teams, which are responsible for staying on time and on budget, but they inadvertently leave themselves carrying the full burden of white space and integration risk. In World Bank projects, as in most complex and strategically critical efforts, these risks can be huge.

When executives assign a team responsibility for a result, however, the team is free—indeed, compelled—to find out what activities will be needed to produce the result and how those activities will fit together. This approach puts white space and integration risk onto the shoulders of the people doing the work. That's appropriate because, as they work, they can discover on the spot what's working and what's not. And in the end, they are rewarded not for performing a series of tasks but for delivering real value. Their success is correlated with benefits to the organization, which will come not only from implementing known activities but also from identifying and integrating new activities.

The milk productivity team in Nicaragua, for example, found out early on that the quantity of milk production was not the issue. The real problem was quality: Distributors were being forced to dump almost half the milk they had bought due to contamination, spoilage, and other problems. So the challenge was to produce milk acceptable to large distributors and manufacturers that complied with international quality standards. Based on this understanding, the team leader invited a representative of Parmalat, the biggest private company in Nicaragua's dairy sector, to join the team. Collaborating with this customer allowed the team to understand Parmalat's quality standards and thus introduce proper hygiene practices to the milk producers in Leon. The collaboration also identified the need for simple equipment such as a centrifuge that could test the quality of batches quickly.

The quality of milk improved steadily in the initial stage of the effort. But then the team discovered that its goal of tripling sales was in danger due to a logistics problem: There wasn't adequate storage available for the additional Grade A milk now being produced. Rather than invest in refrigeration facilities, the Parmalat team member (now assured of the quality of the milk) suggested that the company conduct collection runs in the area daily rather than twice weekly.

At the end of 120 days, the milk productivity team (renamed the "clean-milking" team) and the other four teams not only achieved their goals but also generated a new appreciation for the discovery process. As team leader Piccioni observed at a follow-up workshop: "I now realize how much of the overall success of the effort depends on people discovering for themselves what goals to set and what to do to achieve them."

What's more, the work is more rewarding for the people involved. It may seem paradoxical, but virtually all the teams we've encountered prefer to work on projects that have results-oriented goals, even though they involve some risk and require some discovery, rather than implement clearly predefined tasks.

The Leadership Balancing Act

Despite the obvious benefits of rapid-results initiatives, few companies should use them to replace the horizontal activities altogether. Because of their economies of scale, horizontal activities are a cost-efficient way to work. And so it is the job of the leadership team to balance rapid-results initiatives with longer-term horizontal activities, help spread insights from team to team, and blend everything into an overall implementation strategy.

In Nicaragua, the vertical teams drew members from the horizontal teams, but these people continued to work on the horizontal streams as well, and each team benefited from the work of the others. So, for example, when the milk productivity team discovered the need to educate farmers in clean-milking practices, the horizontal training team knew to adjust the design of its overall training programs accordingly.

The adhesive-material and office-product company Avery Dennison took a similar approach, creating a portfolio of rapid-results initiatives and horizontal work streams as the basis for its overall growth acceleration strategy. Just over a year ago, the company was engaged in various horizontal activities like new technology investments and market studies. The company was growing, but CEO Phil Neal and his leadership team were not satisfied with the pace. Although growth was a major corporate goal, the company had increased its revenues by only 8% in two years.

In August 2002, Neal and president Dean Scarborough tested the vertical approach in three North American divisions, launching 15 rapid-results teams in a matter of weeks. One was charged with securing one new order for an enhanced product, refined in collaboration with one large customer, within 100 days. Another focused on signing up three retail chains so it could use that experience to develop a methodology for moving into new distribution channels. A third aimed to book several hundred thousand dollars in sales in 100 days by providing—through a collaboration with three other suppliers—all the parts needed by a major customer. By December, it had become clear that the vertical growth initiatives were producing results, and the management team decided to extend the process throughout the company, supported by an extensive employee communication campaign. The horizontal activities continued, but at the same time dozens of teams, involving hundreds of people, started working on rapid-results initiatives. By the end of the first quarter of 2003, these teams yielded more than $8 million in new sales, and the company was forecasting that the initiatives would realize approximately $50 million in sales by the end of the year.

The Diversified Products business of Zurich North America, a division of Zurich Financial Services, has taken a similarly strategic approach. CEO Rob Fishman and chief underwriting officer Gary Kaplan commissioned and launched dozens of rapid-results initiatives between April 1999 and December 2002. Their overall long-term objectives were to improve their financial performance and strengthen relationships with core clients. And so they combined vertical teams focused on such goals as increasing payments from a small number of clients for value-added services with horizontal activities targeting staff training, internal processes, and the technology infrastructure. The results were dramatic: In less than four years, loss ratios in the property side of the business dropped by 90%, the expense ratio was cut in half, and fees for value-added services increased tenfold.

Now, when you're managing a portfolio of vertical initiatives and horizontal activities, one of the challenges becomes choosing where to focus the verticals. We generally advise company executives to identify aspects of the effort that they're fairly sure will fail if they are not closely coordinated with one another. We also engage the leadership team in a discussion aimed at identifying other areas of potential uncertainty or risk. Based on those discussions, we ask executives to think of projects that could replicate their longer-term goals on a small scale in a short time and provide the maximum opportunity for learning and discovery.

For instance, at Johnson & Johnson's pharmaceutical R&D group, Thomas Kirsch, the head of global quality assurance, needed to integrate the QA functions for two traditionally autonomous clinical R&D units whose people were located around the world. Full integration was a major undertaking that would unfold over many years, so in addition to launching an extensive series of horizontal activities like developing training standards and devising a system for standardizing currently disparate automated reports, Kirsch also assigned rapid-results teams to quickly put in place several standard operating procedures (SOPs) that cut across the horizontal work streams. The rapid-results teams were focused on the areas he perceived would put the company in the greatest danger of failing to comply with U.S. and European regulations and also on areas where he saw opportunities to generate knowledge that could be applied companywide. There's no science to this approach; it's an iterative process of successive approximation, not a cut-and-dried analytical exercise.

In fact, there are really no "wrong" choices when it comes to deciding which rapid-results initiatives to add to the portfolio. In the context of a large-scale, multiyear, high-stakes effort, each 100-day initiative focused on a targeted result is a relatively low-risk investment. Even if it does not fully realize its goal, the rapid-results initiative will produce valuable lessons and help further illuminate the path to the larger objective. And it will suggest other, and perhaps better-focused, targets for rapid results.

A Call for Humility

Rapid-results initiatives give some new responsibilities to frontline team members while challenging senior leaders to cede control and rethink the way they see themselves. Zurich North America's Gary Kaplan found that the process led him to reflect on his role. "I had to learn to let go: Establishing challenging goals and giving others the space to figure out what it takes to achieve these . . . did not come naturally to me."

Attempting to achieve complex goals in fast-moving and unpredictable environments is humbling. Few leaders and few organizations have figured out how to do it consistently. We believe that a starting point for greater success is shedding the blueprint model that has implicitly driven executive behavior in the management of major efforts. Managers expect they will be able to identify, plan for, and influence all the variables and players in advance, but they can't. Nobody is that smart or has that clear a crystal ball. They can, however, create an ongoing process of learning and discovery, challenging the people close to the action to produce results—and unleashing the organization's collective knowledge and creativity in pursuit of discovery and achievement.

Originally published in September 2003
Reprint R0309H

New Projects

Beware of False Economies

DAVID DAVIS

Executive Summary

NEW PROJECTS, ESPECIALLY those involving high technology, are prone to cost overruns that may double, treble, or even quadruple the original estimates. Companies often find themselves in a nightmare situation, one that doesn't go away even if they manage to finally get the project up and running. Desperate measures taken to stem the hemorrhage of funds during development, such as cutting back on contingency programming, can cripple a project for life.

An inadequate design at the start of a project is more often than not the chief cause of an overrun. Then attempts to economize, made in panic, exacerbate the problem. When this happens, senior management should order a thorough reengineering and redesign, then look again at costs, taking into consideration market conditions. If called for, company executives should decide to abandon the project rather than throw good money after bad. This requires a corporate environment that rewards honest appraisal and courage in its project managers.

THE NEW PLANT HAS HAD a 100% cost overrun and an eight-month completion delay, and now, six months after start-up, it runs at less than half the capacity planned in the original design. The work force is disgruntled after a series of production crises, the customers are increasingly impatient, the original project manager has been fired, and the plant manager is feeling shaky.

Such a situation, unfortunately, describes the fate of many new projects in recent years. Capital expenditure overruns and poor performance are symptoms of a widespread disease affecting pioneer projects. Research reports on new projects verify the general impression that estimates of their performance, timetables, and costs are extraordinarily accident-prone, particularly when they involve new technology. In Britain the disease has a name, the "Concorde syndrome," honoring the airplane project that overran its estimated budget by several thousand percent. The name may differ elsewhere, but the phenomenon is the same. In the United States nuclear power plant overruns are highly publicized. Rarely anywhere does a new project, especially a high-tech undertaking, come on-line on time, on budget, and up to scratch.

A Rand Corporation study on pioneer process plants chronicles this problem.[1] Although the Rand study focuses on pioneer technologies only in the energy industry, it serves as a useful indication of pioneer plants' lack-luster performance because of poor design. The data show, for instance, that the first estimates of the construction cost of pioneer process plants are typically less than half the eventual cost and many are in the range of only one-third. Very few are accurate to within 20%.

The Rand report demonstrates unequivocally that the errors in cost estimates for new plants were dramatically greater when the estimates were based on vague rather than detailed design specifications. When the estimates were generated on the basis of R&D data, the average project eventually overran its budget by more than 100%. As one might expect, as the level of project definition and the quantity of engineering data increase, the overrun declines to about 10% at a fully costed design stage. Attempts to save time and money on initial planning and definition, because of haste or lack of an adequately sized design department, or insufficient funds, are always disastrous.

PIMS data corroborate the results of this Rand report.[2] These findings derive from a study of a large number of start-up ventures involving many companies in a diverse set of industries. Since the PIMS information shows the performance of new projects in terms of achieved market share versus plan, rather than production volume versus design capacity, the findings are not perfectly comparable with those of the Rand study. Volume and market share, however, and design output and plan are sufficiently analogous to indicate a high degree of corroboration.

The PIMS studies forcefully show that the single-industry Rand data are not unique to energy endeavors but apply equally to other industries. Their data show that the typical new project falls a long way short of plan; more than 80% of the projects investigated failed to achieve estimated market share.

The internal responses to the news that expenditures are getting out of control are also remarkably similar. Managers are creatures of habit, and they almost always panic when cost overruns mount. Their fright is understandable since overruns of new projects, especially those involving new technology, often double or triple original estimates, run into many millions of dollars, and can irrevocably damage the careers of those responsible.

In panic, project managers desperately search for budget items to cut. This coping response is effective for a small overrun—say one of 25%—but doesn't work for a large overrun where there isn't enough slack to realize the necessary economies. What the organization faces in such circumstances is not an overrun but a gross original underestimate. No amount of after-the-fact savings can bring the project within its hopelessly unrealistic budget.

Project managers, nevertheless, attempt to solve the problem by making cuts. In general, they rarely perceive hardware cuts—buildings, materials, equipment—as feasible. Rather, they see as the easiest areas to cut those with the least obvious benefits—managerial and design overhead, process control software, equipment quality assurance programs, and test procedures. Ironically, these are the very areas whose costs are often underestimated in the first place.

The favorite candidates for cuts tend to be all those areas that are poorly understood, such as systems and software, quality assurance, and test programs. Project managers often view instrumentation as peripheral to the main process and trim it back, thus changing the operation from a controlled exercise to a gamble. Such gambles rarely pay off: lack of instrumentation at a critical moment can stop a factory. Intangible systems gone wrong can have very tangible results.

How Serious Is the Overrun?

How can management spot a serious overrun in its early stages? Managers cannot, of course, relax budget guidelines every time a project overruns nor can they precipitate a lengthy investigation at every turn of new project development. Just because a project doesn't involve high technology doesn't mean it's safe either; high-tech industries are not the only ones that suffer this problem.

Most capital-intensive investments are high risk because the exit barriers and the high investment levels make it extraordinarily difficult to achieve the profits necessary to earn the requisite return. The expected average ROI for start-up ventures is near zero in the first five years, and ROIs are often negative for the first three or four years. Capital-intensive projects create pressures both on costing and on the effective functioning of the new project after it starts up.

A complex new venture creates many problems for a company. Complex in this context does not necessarily mean high technology—although it often does—for complexity is very much in the eye of the beholder. What is complex for one company may not be for another, because of differences in size, experience, and type of industry. Newness is a good yardstick. If your company is contemplating a major investment project that involves a new technology, market, or a size new to the company, serious over runs are a real possibility.

When an overrun threatens, the questions to ask are simple.

In your industry, does the project involve pioneer technology?

If the technology is not pioneer, is it new to your company? Has any of your project managers implemented this type of project before?

Is the project much bigger than any your company has handled before?

Was the project costed before the design was completed?

In regard to the last question, the Rand study showed that a surprisingly large number of pioneer projects have their budgets agreed on before completion of the final design. No doubt this practice is partly the result of the planning timetables of large organizations. Detailed design is an expensive process that is often delayed until management and the board of directors approve the project. The Rand study demonstrates unequivocally that the sketchier the design at budget approval time, the larger the overrun.

What often happens in preliminary design is a frugal approach is taken that turns out to be penny-wise but pound-foolish. A feasibility study, based on inadequate detail, forms the basis of the proposal sent to the board of directors. Project managers base cost estimates on guesses and don't attempt to test the validity of their appraisals by drawing up detailed specifications and asking for bids. In the case of a new-to-company project, a feasibility study often simply takes the cost of a similar plant or process used elsewhere and adds an inflation factor. It does not, for example, study compatibility of the preliminary design with local materials or the environment.

Although a company by this procedure may save the expense of a full design at an early stage of a proposal—and therefore expenses on proposals that never get off the ground—the ramifications of committing capital to a project on the basis of a sketchy feasibility study are enormous.

If, as a manager, you find that a project your company is developing has gone well beyond its estimates and the answer to any of the three questions on its newness is yes, it is probable that you have a serious overrun. If the answer to question four concerning the use of a feasibility study is also yes, then it is highly likely that you have a serious overrun arising from incorrect estimates.

What to Do

An overrun usually puts lower and middle managers in an inescapable box because they don't have the necessary decision-making powers. In most cases, only senior executives are in a position to take action.

Although the usual routine of "retrench, retrieve, revise, and review" is useful in dealing with overruns, management should instigate the following procedures when the problem is serious.

VERIFY THE NATURE OF THE PROBLEM

Senior managers' most important task in dealing with a budget-breaking project—and indeed with any project—is creating a corporate environment that encourages honest and frank disclosure. Everyone concerned with the project must be prepared to recognize and announce serious snags when they become evident. This can be difficult, especially when the first sign of failure precipitates a search for a scapegoat. Only senior management can set the tone for an environment of openness essential for the recovery of a project taking the wrong road.

The ways in which senior executives choose to discourage cover-ups and recriminations depend on their management styles. Some companies accept errors of judgment as the inevitable consequence of high-risk activity; top officers do not react to bad decisions in a punitive manner so long as the perpetrators deal with their mistakes promptly and do not repeat them. In such a regime, concealment of a problem is the cardinal sin that is punished harshly.

Another company's approach might resemble the "no surprises" management style at ITT under Harold Geneen, who insisted on early quantitative analysis in excruciating detail and on follow-up thoroughness on a scale rarely seen elsewhere. This kind of tough, unforgiving management style with its insistence on extreme detail can work only if project managers either get it right the first time or react with utmost honesty when a project starts to slip.

Other managers keep new ventures under control through powerful operations audit departments that check major projects thoroughly at each stage, beginning with the first budgets. The control mechanism a company chooses to oversee new projects should, of course, fit its corporate structure and management methods.

However it goes about it, a company should develop the means to identify early on whether an overrun is a major or a minor problem. Most disasters start as a series of 10% slippages, so it is essential to have access to the data necessary to judge the nature of these failures to meet estimate deadlines. The standard technique of increasing the budget pressure has at least a chance of curbing bona fide 10% overruns. Serious overruns require more drastic measures, and the sooner these are taken, the better.

REENGINEER THE PROJECT

Since the cause of most serious overruns is an inadequate initial design, an important step in dealing with the problem is to reengineer the project as comprehensively as possible.

What management hopes to accomplish by reengineering is the identification and rectification of errors that resulted from proceeding with the project on the basis of a skimpy feasibility study with many unknowns and inaccurate estimates.

Company X provides a good example of the need for realistic, in-depth initial costing. This young company in a high-technology industry embarked on a large program involving two capital-intensive projects with complex technology and a high level of computer control. One project, completed at the end of 1981, was a classic case of a unit overrun that came on stream some 100% over estimate. Competitive considerations led to the initiation of another project before the first, disastrous project was operational.

With only a few differences in personnel, the same management group was responsible for both ventures. Each project involved a technology that was new to the management group and that had a history of difficulty in start-ups elsewhere. The company planned to link the computer controls for the two projects, but each was to have its own hardware and software.

Project 1 was costed before the design was completed, which was a particularly bad error because the technology was new. As a result its costing was hopelessly wrong. Parts of the budget overran from the very first day, sometimes by several hundred percent. This put intense pressure on costs throughout the development of the project, which in turn impaired Project 1's functioning after start-up.

In contrast, Project 2 was conceived and implemented in calmer circumstances. The top managers realized intuitively (although they were not talking about it) that something was dramatically wrong with how Project 1 was being handled, so they strengthened the management group by adding a planner experienced in the relationship between design and budget.

Before submitting the costing for Project 2 to the board of directors for approval, the group undertook a $250,000 full design through to quotations. Subsequently, although pressures on costs arose during development, these were far less frenetic than in the case of Project 1.

The effect of the different approaches to costing on the operational effectiveness of the projects was dramatic. Project 2 reached 90% of design output in 3 months or less, whereas Project 1 had reached only 60% of design output at the end of 24 months.

The statistical significance of the difference in performance of the two projects is shown in the exhibit "Performance of Two Major Projects Against Rand Report Data," which compares the performance of Project 1 and Project 2 with the average performance (as a percentage of design capacity) of the pioneer process plants in the Rand report. In terms of the Rand average, during the first year of operations, Project 1's performance fell 20%

below the average of pioneer plants, and Project 2's performance, for the most part, was 20% above average.

Although the Rand study covered a single industry only, the PIMS data show that the operational effectiveness of new projects, measured by market penetration, is considerably less than plan irrespective of industry for many years of the project life (see the exhibit "Market Penetration, Planned vs. Actual").

IDENTIFY UNDERESTIMATED AREAS

An engineering review enables management to spot areas where ignorance governs decisions. Such areas always exist with new projects, although the people connected with their development rarely admit it. Almost without

Performance of Two Major Projects Against Rand Report Data

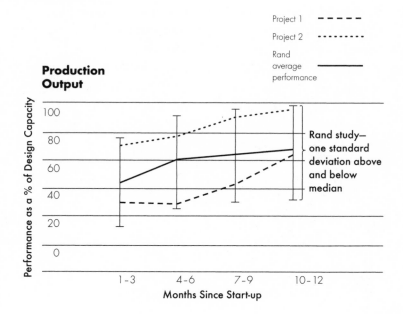

Project 1   – – – –
Project 2   · · · · · · · ·
Rand average performance   ——————

exception, the costs in these areas are underestimated, and they are first in line for cutting at budget review.

One area reasonably representative of poor under-standing in many complex modern plants is process control programming. It is used as an example several times in this article since it highlights so well both the causes and effects of designer and managerial ignorance. Companies going into ventures in which they are inexperienced are apt to be unaware of the cost and importance of adequate programming. They tend to neglect, or even ignore, the need for:

Intensive contingency programming and interaction checking. It is very straightforward—and inexpensive—to program for a linear series of events, but

---

Market Penetration, Planned vs. Actual

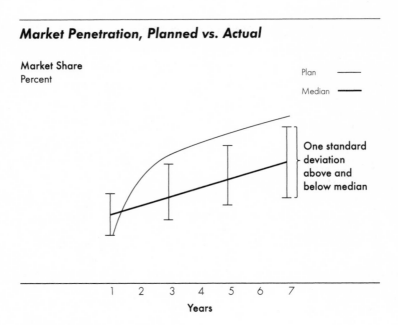

Market Share
Percent

Plan ⎯⎯⎯

Median ▬▬▬

One standard deviation above and below median

Years

1   2   3   4   5   6   7

Source: Derived from PIMS published data

much more difficult—and expensive—to plan for the possible interactions in a modern factory.

Projects with inadequate contingency programs can end up in a lot of trouble, especially with interactions based on automatic controls. Most automatically controlled factories have systems able to operate within microseconds of each other that can overwhelm other systems and subsystems in the plant. A project must have built-in contingency programs that guard against these and other interactions.

An example of what automatic controls can do that caught the popular imagination was the tiny fail-safe device in the Sir Adam Beck power station at Niagara Falls that tripped out on a cold November night in 1965 and, in 2.7 seconds, blacked out virtually the whole northeast United States and Canada.

An intensive "human programming" effort. It is hard enough to plan for a multiplicity of mechanical and electronic interactions without taking human responses into account. Nevertheless, new projects need systems that are robust in the face of the full scope of human reactions, ranging from the late-night languor of the back shift to the panic that occurs when the console unexpectedly lights up. The accident at Three Mile Island demonstrated this need in a macabre way.

As a rule of thumb, to have a reasonable probability of success, a process control program must cover more than 95% of all possible events.

A thorough series of process simulation tests. Mistakes are inevitable in the design and development of new projects—particularly in high-tech projects— given the complexity of the systems involved. Process simulation tests can identify likely mistakes, but devising tests that deal with human, mechanical, and electronic interactions in the context of an incomplete project is difficult as well as time-consuming and costly.

Moreover, not all the failures will be found at the testing stage. It is necessary, therefore, that programming be designed in a manner that will permit diagnosis of potential and actual problems once the project is up and running.

Company X's Project 1 took a linear-logic approach, whereas Project 2 had built-in contingency programs to take complex interactions into account. Although it is impossible to quantify all the costs of delays and malfunctions, control system failures after start-up in Project 1 cost the equivalent in lost earnings of between six months' and one year's production. At a 15% discount rate, assuming that tax has minimal effect, losing one year's production at the beginning of a project's life is the same as adding 15% to the project cost. To put it another way, assuming a ten-year project life, a 20% residual value, and a high sales-investment ratio of 3 to 1, these delays are equivalent to a 1% cut in sales revenue over the life of a project. At a more usual new project sales-investment ratio of 1 to 1, the effect is the same as a sales revenue reduction of 3% for the project life (see the exhibit "Price Effect Equivalent for a One Year Delay in Start-up").

These monetary losses do not take into account the effects on the company of disappointed customers, an atmosphere of failure in both the work force and management, a poor reputation in the industry and with competitors, and lack of enthusiasm on the part of investors.

AVOID FALSE SOLUTIONS

The typical response to an overrun is to cut costs wherever this seems possible. But this reaction can create, in the end, an even greater disaster if the overrun is caused by inadequate original costing in areas subsequently further starved of funds. In a desperate gamble to keep a project alive, managers can cripple a venture.

To carry on with the example of process control programming, cutting back on software investment is often seen as a good way to cheesepare project costs. The cause for this increasingly common harmful decision is the difficulty many managers have in assessing the value of intangible budget items. Like other factors critical to the cost, performance, and profit of new projects, software has several characteristics that attract budget cutters:

Price Effect Equivalent for a One Year Delay in Start-up

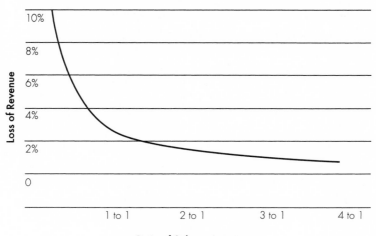

It is intangible.

Its importance is not easily quantified.

Project engineers and managers often understand poorly its use and value.

Managers perceive it to be expensive.

Moreover, cutting software investment during development of a project can have high leverage on its eventual operational effectiveness.

As we have seen, Company X's two projects provided some hard data on the effect of cutting back on software investment, as well as represented extremes of method. Project 1 used a minimum-cost approach to process software, limiting the planned expenditures to 19% of hardware cost; Project 2 raised the investment to 43%. The difference, therefore, was one of attitude to software as shown in expenditure level.

The level of software costs of both projects in the end were identical—45% of hardware costs. But as noted earlier, the operational effectiveness of Project 2 was much better than that of Project 1, especially during the first year of operation. This functional superiority did not arise solely from better software development, of course. But managers should recognize that high levels of software effectiveness are a prerequisite for outstanding performance by new projects.

Managers cannot blithely carry on spending money on intangibles in a badly overrun project. The characteristics that led to the selection of software for budget cuts—the expensive, poorly quantified, and poorly understood nature of the material—are shared by many other areas such as quality assurance programs, test routines, and training. But these are usually necessary for the viability of a project and cutting them out or cheeseparing their costs is not the answer to an over-run. Like software, these aspects of a project have high leverage on its eventual effectiveness.

The effect of software cuts during the development of Project 1 was that some 1% of total project costs were deferred, but not saved, at an eventual extra cost to the project in excess of 10% of total costs. In this case, a deferral of a few hundred thousand dollars resulted in further costs of many millions of dollars. See "False Assumptions" at the end of this article for a fictionalized account of a false solution.

RECOST THE ENTIRE PROJECT

Rather than make irrational budget cuts of intangible items, what managers should do, once reengineering and a new design are complete, is to recost the new project on the basis of the latest design and review the market position for the project's products. Now it will be possible to make more accurate forecasts of external variables.

The reengineering exercise should have entailed a detailed design review, or even redesign, and should have included a thorough operational analysis that highlighted all doubtful or poorly understood areas. The objective study of the project must now take a hard look at costs. What will be necessary is detailed costing of all changed areas and probably recosting of the whole project.

Cost estimates at this time will also reflect changes in prices of materials and labor arising not only from differences in supplier markets but also from the experience gained during the implementation of the original design in terms of amendments and alterations of specifications.

The recosting should take into account an unbiased review of profit potential for the project, including those areas shown by the PIMS study to be often poorly estimated—market share and overall volume of market, pricing of the product output, and marketing expenses.

The difficulty of abandoning a project after several million dollars have already been committed to it tends to prevent objective review and recosting. For this reason, ideally an independent management team—one not involved in the project's development —should do the recosting and, if possible, the entire review. When the technology involved is new to the company but already in use elsewhere, it is always worthwhile to try to bring in a strong, outside technical management team well-versed in the technology to undertake this study.

ABANDON IF NECESSARY

If the numbers do not hold up in the review and recosting, the company should abandon the project. The number of bad projects that make it to the operational stage serve as proof that their supporters often balk at this decision.

There are a number of reasons for irrational behavior at this critical point, including many things that senior management can do little about. Obsessive enthusiasm by project managers, fascination with novelty and technology, and the good, old-fashioned need to achieve are important driving forces in any project. Under most circumstances it would be inadvisable to suppress these motivators; channeling of enthusiasm must be done carefully.

It is a brave manager who recommends the abandonment of a project under his command after a commitment of $20 million. Project managers who believe that closing down a project will wreck their careers are tempted to carry on in the hope they will have a slight chance of saving their reputations. Both courses carry the risk of disaster for those responsible for a project, but one—abandonment—is often far better for the company.

Senior managers need to create an environment that rewards honesty and courage and provides for more decision making on the part of project managers. Companies must have an atmosphere that encourages projects to succeed, but executives must also allow them to fail.

Starting new projects is fraught with risk. Costs may escalate and operational capabilities may decline as a project develops and goes on stream. Inadequate early cost estimates and improper budgeting increase risks and often lead to enormous overruns. The usual response to burgeoning expenses—to tighten budgets in intangible areas—leads to false economies that can cripple the operational capabilities of a project and will probably not save money after all.

When an overrun becomes serious, the only sensible recourse is to rework the project from the ground up and, if necessary, either abandon or rebudget. Minor cost cutting to buy time is counterproductive. Although false economies involving programming and other "soft-cost" areas may generate confidence or complacency, they do not solve any problems.

Decisions to reengineer, recost, and perhaps give up are hard to make. It is essential that senior managers monitor what is happening with new projects and be prepared to shoulder the difficult decisions themselves.

False Assumptions

SHE TOOK OFF HER WRAPS in front of the mirror, for the sake of one last glance at herself in all her glory. But suddenly she uttered a cry. The diamonds were no longer round her neck. . . .

She turned to her husband in horror. "I . . . I've . . . lost Madame Forestier's necklace." . . .

Loisel had eighteen thousand francs left to him by his father. The balance of the sum he proposed to borrow. He raised loans in all quarters, a thousand francs from one man, five hundred from another, five louis here, three louis there. He gave promissory notes, agreed to exorbitant terms, had dealings with usurers, and with all the money-lending hordes. He compromised his whole future, and had to risk his signature, hardly knowing if he would be able to honour it. . . . At the end of ten years, they had paid off everything to the last penny. . . .

One Sunday Madame Loisel went for a stroll in the Champs-Élysées and caught sight of Madame Forestier. . . . Now that the debt was paid, why should she not tell her the whole story? . . .

Madame Forestier stopped dead. "You mean to say that you bought a diamond necklace to replace mine? . . . Oh, my poor, dear Mathilde! Why, mine was only imitation. At the most it was worth five hundred francs!"

Source: From "The Necklace" by Guy de Maupassant

Notes

1. Edward Merrow, Kenneth Phillips, and Christopher Myers, *Understanding Cost Growth and Performance Shortfalls in Pioneer Process Plants* (Santa Barbara, CA: Rand Corporation, 1981).

2. Data presented as "Findings on Start-up Ventures," at the PIMS Membership Conference, Boston, MA, 1981.

Originally published in March–April 1985
Reprint 85203

The Return Map

Tracking Product Teams

CHARLES H. HOUSE AND RAYMOND L. PRICE

Executive Summary

WITH A NEW PRODUCT, time is now more valuable than money. The costs of conceiving and designing a product are less important to its ultimate success than timeliness to market.

One of the most important ways to speed up product development is through interfunctional teamwork. The "Return Map," developed at Hewlett-Packard, provides a way for people from different functions to triangulate on the product development process as a whole. It graphically represents the contributions of all team members to the moment when a project breaks even. It forces the team to estimate and re-estimate the time it will take to perform critical tasks, so that products can get out fast. It subjects the team to the only discipline that works, namely, self-discipline.

The map is, in effect, a graph representing time and money, where the time line is divided into three phases: investigation, development, and manufacturing and sales. Meanwhile, costs are plotted against time—as are revenues when they are realized after manufacturing release. Within these points of reference, four novel metrics emerge: Break-Even-Time, Time-to-Market, Break-Even-After-Release, and the Return Factor. All metrics are estimated at the beginning of a project to determine its feasibility, then they are tracked carefully while the project evolves to determine its success.

Missed forecasts are inevitable, but managers who punish employees for missing their marks will only encourage them to estimate conservatively, thus building slack into a system meant to eliminate slack. Estimates are a team responsibility, and deviations provide valuable information that spurs continuous investigation and improvement.

ONCE TIME WAS MONEY. Now it is more valuable than money. A McKinsey study reports that, on average, companies lose 33% of after-tax profit when they ship products six months late, as compared with losses of 3.5% when they overspend 50% on product development. More and more, advanced manufacturers are learning that the time required to develop a new product has more influence on its success than its costs.

Little wonder, then, that senior managers are working hard to reduce their new product development cycles. At Hewlett-Packard, well over 50% of sales come from products introduced during the past three years, and more than 500 product development projects are going on at any given time. Even enterprises that develop just a few new products over several years, like Boeing Commercial Airplane Group, are focusing on reducing the time required to develop them.

It is a common belief in management practice today that one of the most effective ways to shorten development cycles is through the collaborative work of cross-functional development teams. But if anything is easier said than done, it is that marketing people, development engineers, and manufacturing engineers should collaborate rather than "throw product specifications over the wall" to one another.

Collaboration among people from different functions is difficult, uncertain, and suffers from too little mutual understanding. New product development teams are typically composed of people who do not have the experience or qualifications to criticize each other's judgments or performance—certainly not while the project is evolving. They do not, and cannot, know all that their colleagues from other functions know. And uncertainty comes in many forms. What features do customers want? How do features translate into sales? Is the technology available to develop the features? Will the product be manufacturable at the desired price? Much of the challenge of new product development is centered on people from different functions finding answers to, and getting agreement on, just such questions.

Obviously, the more team members understand the work of other functions and the interrelationships among all functions, the more likely they are to make intelligent decisions that will enhance the success of the product. But what constitutes understanding? Bill Hewlett, a founder of Hewlett-Packard, used to say, "You cannot manage what you cannot measure," and his

corollary was "What gets measured gets done." By infer-
ence, the real challenge for teams is to develop measures
that will help individuals assess how well they are doing
what they agree must be done. Advanced manufacturers
must create new products that will make the most profit
in the least time, but what metric can managers of interfunctional teams use to direct their employees' efforts
toward this outcome?

Ideally, such a metric would encourage the ongoing
monitoring of a new product development project. It
would allow people from different disciplines to assess
the impact of their decisions and their colleagues' decisions on the entire project. The metric would encourage
collaboration among different functions: engender challenge and criticism without encouraging presumptuous-
ness. It would serve as a prompt for learning and
improvement. It would be easy to read and interpret,
something to sketch on the back of an envelope while in
a coffeepot discussion. And it would provide a way of
visualizing progress holistically.

In fact, Hewlett-Packard has been using just such a
metric since 1987—we named it the "Return Map"—and
it is so simple and elegant that it has become a staple of
the company's product development cycle. The Return
Map graphically represents the contributions of all team
members to product success in terms of time and
money. First and foremost, it includes the critical elements of product development—the investment in product development and the return or profits from that
investment. But the Return Map also shows the elapsed
time to develop the product, introduce it, and achieve
the returns.

Not surprisingly, the Return Map's crucial coordinate
is the point at which product sales generate sufficient

profit to pay back the initial development investment, that is, when the project breaks even. But the map's greatest virtue is not in what it says so much as in what it does. It provides a superordinate goal and measure for all the functions and thus shifts the team's focus from "who is responsible" to "what needs to get done." Even more important, the map forces members of the team to estimate and reestimate the time and money it will take to complete their tasks and the impact of their actions on overall project success. In giving a comprehensive picture of the common task, it helps to create the only discipline that works, namely, self-discipline.

The Basic Elements

The Return Map is intended to be used by all of the functional managers on the business team. Basically, it is a two dimensional graph displaying time and money on the x and y axes respectively. The x axis is usually drawn on a linear scale, while the y axis is drawn most effectively on a logarithmic scale because for successful products the difference between sales and investment costs will be greater than 100:1. It is important to remember when looking at the exhibit curves that the dollar amounts are rising cumulatively. The x axis is divided into three segments, showing partitioned tasks and responsibilities—Investigation, Development, and Manufacturing and Sales (see the exhibit "The Return Map Captures Both Money and Time").

The purpose of Investigation is to determine the desired product features, the product's cost and price, the feasibility of the proposed technologies, and the plan for product development and introduction. At this point, all numbers are estimates. Investigation is usually the

The Return Map Captures Both Money and Time

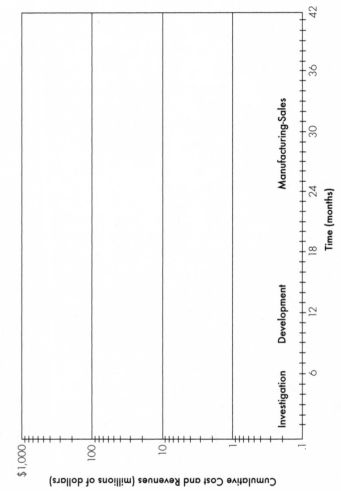

Investigation   Development   Manufacturing-Sales

Time (months)

Cumulative Cost and Revenues (millions of dollars)

$1,000

100

10

1

.1

6   12   18   24   30   36   42

responsibility of a small team and requires a relatively modest investment. Obviously, Marketing and R&D should collaborate to determine what features customers want and how they could be provided. At the end of Investigation, the company commits to develop a product with specific features using agreed-upon technologies.

The Development phase is usually the primary domain of R&D in consultation with manufacturing; its purpose is to determine how to produce the product at the desired price. Challenges during this phase include changing product features, concurrent design of the product and the manufacturing processes, and, often, the problems associated with doing something that has not been done before.

The formal end of the Development phase is Manufacturing Release (MR)—that is, when the company commits to manufacture and sell the product. When the product is ready to be manufactured and shipped to customers, sales become a reality and manufacturing, marketing, sales costs, and profits are finally more than estimates. The transitions between these phases or the project checkpoints are key times for the Return Map.

Perhaps the best way to grasp how the Return Map evolves from these early stages is to examine a map for a completed project, where all the variables are known—in this case, the map for a recent Hewlett-Packard pocket calculator (see the exhibit "First, the Team Plots Estimates").

Investigation took 4 months and cost about $400,000; Development required 12 months and $4.5 million, with many new manufacturing process designs for higher quality and higher production volumes. Hence, the total product development effort from beginning to manufacturing and sales release took 16 months and cost $4.9

First, the Team Plots Estimates

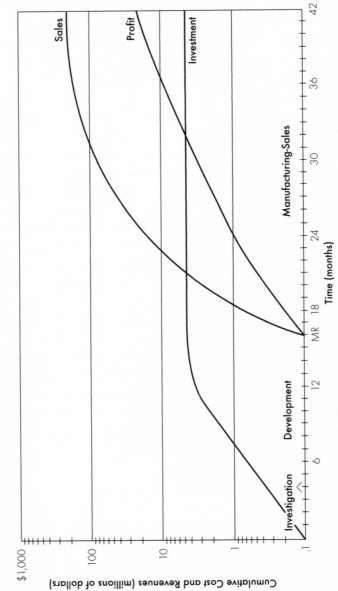

million (see the investment line on the exhibit). Once the product was released, sales increased consistently for 5 months and then increased at a slightly faster pace during the next 9 months. Sales volume for the first year was $56 million and for the second year was $145 million (see the sales line on the exhibit—and remember, the differences are greater than they appear owing to the log scale). Cumulative sales volume gives a sense of how quickly and effectively the product was introduced and sold.

In the first year, net profits of $2.2 million were less than expected due to the sales volume lag and the resulting increase in cost per unit. But profits (see the profit line in the exhibit) increased significantly in the second year and passed through the investment line about 16 months after Manufacturing Release. For the second year, net profits reached $13 million. Profits are the best indicator of the contribution the product made to the customers since they reflect both the total volume of sales and the price the product can command in the marketplace.

So the critical lines that are systematically plotted on the Return Map include new product investment dollars, sales dollars, and profit dollars. Each of these is plotted as both time and money, with money in total cumulative dollars. Now that we have the basic elements of the map, we can focus on some novel metrics.

New Metrics

The map tracks—in dollars and months—R&D and manufacturing investment, sales, and profit. At the same time, it provides the context for new metrics: Break-Even-Time, Time-to-Market, Break-Even-After-Release, and the Return Factor. These four metrics (see the exhibit "Key Metrics Complete the Picture," plotted for the pocket calculator) become the focus of management reviews, functional performance discussions, learning, and most important, they are the basis for judging overall product success.

Break-Even-Time, or *BET*, is the key metric. It is defined as the time from the start of investigation until product profits equal the investment in development. In its simplest form, BET is a measure of the total time until the break-even point on the original investment; for the pocket calculator, BET is 32 months. BET is the one best measure for the success of the whole product development effort because it conveys a sense of urgency about time; it shows the race to generate sufficient profit to justify the product in the first place.

Time-to-Market, or *TM*, is the total development time from the start of the Development phase to Manufacturing Release. For the calculator project, TM was 12 months. This time and its associated costs are determined primarily by R&D efficiency and productivity. TM makes visible the major check-points of Investigation and Development. It is obviously the most important R&D measure.

Break-Even-After-Release, or *BEAR*, is the time from Manufacturing Release until the project investment costs are recovered in product profit. BEAR for the calculator was 16 months. This measure focuses on how efficiently the product was transferred to marketing and manufacturing and how effectively it was introduced to the marketplace. Just as TM is considered the most important R&D metric, BEAR is the most important measure for marketing and manufacturing.

Finally, the *Return Factor*, or *RF*, is a calculation of profit dollars divided by investment dollars at a specific

Key Metrics Complete the Picture

Cumulative Cost and Revenues (millions of dollars)

$1,000

100

10

1

.1

Investigation

Development

Manufacturing-Sales

Time-to-Market (TM)

Break-Even-Time (BET)

Return Factor (RF) = .45 (1 year after MR)

Break-Even-After-Release (BEAR)

RF = 3.1 (2 years after MR)

Sales

Profit

Investment

Time (months)

6   12   MR   18   24   30   36   42

point in time after a product has moved into manufacturing and sales. In the case of the pocket calculator, RF
after one year was .45 (that is, cumulative profit of $2.2
million divided by total investment of $4.9 million) and
was 3.1 (a profit of $15.2 million divided by $4.9 million)
after two years. The RF gives an indication of the total
return on the investment without taking into account
how long it took to achieve that return.

The effectiveness of the Return Map hinges on the
involvement of all three major functional areas in the
development and introduction of new products. The
map captures the link between the development team
and the rest of the company and the customer. If the
product does not sell and make money, for whatever reasons, the product development efforts were wasted. The
team is accountable for designing and building products
that the customers want, doing it in a timely manner,
and effectively transferring the products to the rest of
the company.

Making the Most of the Return Map

We have argued that an interfunctional team uses the
Return Map most appropriately during the Investigation
phase by generating estimates for a final map, including
investment, sales, and profit. These initial estimates or
forecasts are a "stake in the ground" for the team and
will be used for comparison and learning throughout the
project. By focusing on the accuracy of the forecasts,
marketing, R&D, and manufacturing are forced to examine problems as a team; all three functions are thus sharing the burden of precision.

Too often, the whole burden during the initial phase
of a project is placed on the R&D team—to generate
schedules, functionality, and cost goals. But the Return

Map requires accurate sales forecasts, which forces market researchers to get better and better at competitive analysis, customer understanding, and market development. Similarly, manufacturing involvement is essential for forecasting cost and schedule goals; manufacturing engineers should never be left to develop the manufacturing process after the design is set.

We cannot emphasize enough that missed forecasts generated for the Return Map in the Investigation phase should be viewed as valuable information, comparable with defect rates in manufacturing—deviations from increasingly knowable standards, proof that either the process is out of whack or the means for setting the standard are. The Return Map can be used to provide a visual perspective on sales forecasts and expected profits given any number of hypothetical scenarios. What if the forecasts varied by 20%, over or under? What are the implications of reaching mature sales six months earlier than expected? The Return Map allows for a kind of graphic sensitivity analysis of product development and introduction decisions; it sets the stage for further, indeed, continual investigation.

By no means should the Return Map be used by management to punish people whose forecasts prove inaccurate. Estimates are a team responsibility or at least a functional one—no individual should be held responsible for generating the information on which they are based. Moreover, if functions are penalized for being late, they will simply learn to estimate conservatively, building slack into a discipline whose very purpose is the elimination of slack.

Consider the estimated Return Map for a proposed ultrasound machine (see the exhibit "During Investigation, the Ultrasound Team Makes Early Estimates"). The Investigation phase is planned to last 5 months and cost

During Investigation, the Ultrasound Team Makes Early Estimates

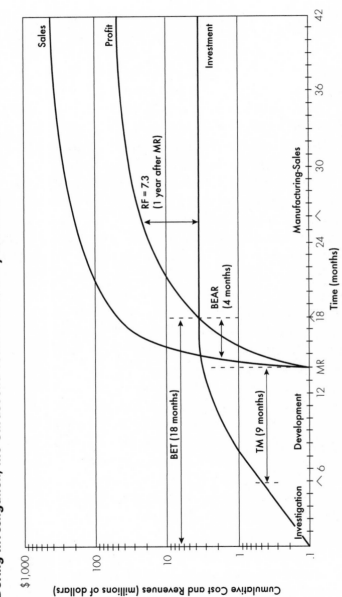

$500,000, TM is estimated to be 9 months and cost $2.3 million, while anticipated BET is 18 months. Mature sales volume is expected to be 300 units a month, or $16 million, and mature profits are expected to be $2 million per month. These estimates were made by a project team that had developed two other ultrasound products and were quite knowledgeable about the medical instrument business. They wanted to take more time in the Investigation phase to completely understand the desired product features in order to move more quickly during the Development phase.

During the Development phase, that is, once product features and the customer requirements are understood, TM becomes vital and other concerns fade. The Return Map implicitly stresses execution now. The faster a product is introduced into a competitive marketplace, the longer potential life it will have—hence the greater its return. TM emphasizes the need to respond to market windows and competitive pressures.

It is difficult to keep project goals focused during development. Creeping features, management redirection, and "new" marketing data all push the project to change things in midstream, much to the detriment of engineering productivity and TM. The Return Map can help put this new information into perspective and help team members analyze the impact of changes on the entire project. For example, how much will new features increase sales and profits? If adding the features delays the introduction of the product, how will that affect sales and profit?

For example, two months into the Development phase of the ultrasound machine, Hewlett-Packard labs had a breakthrough in ultrasound technology that would enable the machine to offer clearer images. Should the project incorporate this new technology or proceed as planned? The project team determined that customers would value the features and they would result in more sales, though the new technology would be more expensive to produce. But would the changes be worth the extra expense?

The original Return Map was updated with a new set of assumptions (see the exhibit "During Development, New Technology Calls for Revised Estimates"). Development costs would increase by 40% to $3.2 million, the TM would be extended by at least 4 months, but the sales could increase by 50% and net profits could increase by 30%. The Return Map demonstrated that the BET for the project would extend to 22 months, the BEAR would remain the same, but the RF would be reduced slightly.

What on the surface seemed like a great idea proved not to increase significantly the economic return. In the end, the team decided to incorporate the new technology anyway, but in order to capture a greater market share, not to make more money. The team went into the changes with its eyes open; it made a strategic decision, not one driven by optimistic numbers.

Once the team gets beyond Investigation, the Development phase, represented by TM, can itself be segmented into subphases and submetrics that provide greater understanding and accuracy and more effective management. Teams that compare projects over time become more and more sophisticated about the development processes underlying TM forecasts. Within Hewlett-Packard, for instance, the time required for printed circuit board turnaround emerged as something of a bottleneck for many projects. So the company developed streamlined processes for printed circuit

During Development, New Technology Calls for Revised Estimates

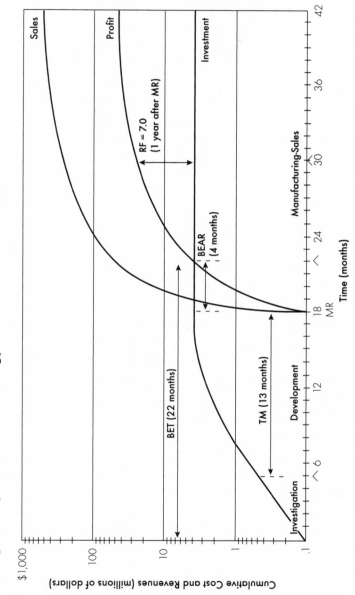

board development and eventually simulation tools that reduced the need for board prototypes.

Another HP study showed that company managers were much more effective at predicting total engineering months than total calendar months (that is, effort rather than time). The big mistake here seemed to be a tendency on the company's part to try to do too many projects with the available engineers—resulting in understaffed projects. Once management focused on staffing projects adequately, the company experienced a significant reduction in this kind of forecast error.

Beyond Manufacturing Release

The Manufacturing Release, or MR, meeting is perhaps the single most important built-in checkpoint in the system. It is structured to allow the management team to focus on the original goals of the entire development effort and to compare the goals at the project's inception with the new estimates based on the realities of the Development phase. The team can now analyze the adjustments required by the marketing and manufacturing estimates, in consequence of any elapsed time, schedule slippages, or the changed competitive and economic scene.

Consider the updated Return Map for the ultrasound project showing the estimates that were made during the Development phase and the real development cost and TM (see the exhibit "At Manufacturing Release, the Team Sees What Actually Happened"). The project took two extra months to complete and cost $700,000 more than estimated. At this time, the estimates for sales and profits are lower than Development phase estimates. The important point for team members to understand,

At Manufacturing Release, the Team Sees What Actually Happened

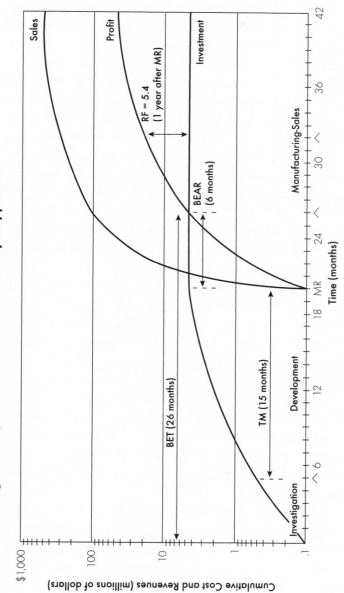

obviously, is the effect of a slide in TM on the other measures, and they should take corrective action in the future to avoid delays. A series of MR meetings, supported by documentation, will sharpen any team's estimating and development skills.

During the Manufacturing and Sales phase, the emphasis shifts from estimates to real data for sales and profits. This is the moment of truth for the development team. As sales and profits vary from the forecast, everyone has the right—and responsibility—to ask why. One HP study tracked sales forecasts for 16 products over a two-year period. The targets were set rather broadly—a 20% deviation either way would be acceptable—on the assumption that manufacturing and sales could adjust successfully to either surging or weakening demand within that range. Nevertheless, only 12% of the forecasts fell into the acceptable range.

From our experience, this is the time when the project team gets the most constructive criticism, insight, and enthusiasm to do things right, now and the next time. At the MR stage, analysis, thoughtfulness, and responsiveness are vital. We have seen products falter because of such varied problems as unreliable performance, an unprepared sales force, or an inability to manufacture the product in appropriate volumes—all problems that should be correctable, even at this late date. Problems such as inappropriate features, high costs, and poor designs, however, will have to wait for the next generation.

Incidentally, one important lesson we have learned is the need to keep a nucleus of the project team together for at least six months after introduction. Team members should be available to help smooth the transition to full production and sales, and the company's next generation of products will benefit greatly from the team's collective learning.

In addition to helping manage and analyze individual products, the Return Map can be used for families of products, programs, and major systems. As companies establish a market presence with a product, it must be buttressed with corresponding products based on customer requirements and the next appropriate technologies. A complete program strategy for an important market usually embraces products from three overlapping generations, which we call a "strategic cycle."

A family of products can lead to overall success, even if some of the products do not reach standard return goals and are not seen as successful. The success of major new programs may not be obvious until the second generation is produced: it may take many years before success or failure is completely determined.

The table "Three Generations of One Product Family" illustrates the cumulative data for an entire product family, divided into three generations, with the second generation divided into five major products (A,B,C,D,E).

A quick scan of the second generation of products suggests that productivity could have been improved by doing only those products that end up with a low BET, low BEAR, and a high RF. Unfortunately, this requires more luck than foresight. One product in the series (product D) made much of the economic difference, but it is not possible to establish a full program with only one product. In fact, the success of product D was almost entirely dependent on the investment made in the technology for product C (note the long Time-to-Market) and the market understanding gained from product B.

Three Generations of One Product Family

Product	R&D Investment (millions of dollars)	Investigation Time (months)	Time-to-Market (months)	Break-Even-After-Release (months)	Break-Even-Time (months)	Return Factor (months after MR)
Family	$19.0				68	3.1 at 60 months
First Generation	3.0	16	19	27	62	5.0 at 36 months
Second Generation	4.5	10	36	17	63	7.4 at 48 months
A	0.65	10	24	6	40	4.8 at 24 months
B	0.8	0	24	23	47	0.8 at 8 months
C	1.7	12	42	9	63	2.8 at 20 months
D	0.7	12	24	4	40	7.0 at 12 months
E	0.7	12	31	6	49	1.5 at 8 months
Third Generation	11.5	8	36	22	66	4.0 at 72 months

To have a winning and sustained market presence usually requires at least three generations of products. Frequently, one of those generations will develop a new and significant technology, while the next generation will exploit that technology by means of rapid product development cycles—products tailored to specific markets.

Easier Said Than Done

The Return Map, along with its BET, TM, BEAR, and RF measures, provides a useful indicator of the effectiveness of new product development and introduction. It provides a general management tool to track the development process and to take corrective action in real time. But while the map is simple, the difficulties of using it well are great, time-consuming, and require significant commitment. The first challenge is to get the forecast data out and to track the actual costs, sales, and profits against those forecasts. Unfortunately, most development teams will have to pull this data manually from the period expense reports, since most companies track costs, sales, and profits on a period rather than a project basis. If development teams can prove project data useful, though, accounting departments may start tracking numbers for major projects and not only aggregate numbers month by month. (HP is now overhauling its cost accounting systems to provide project as well as period data.)

Another challenge is to get functional managers to work together toward common goals and to share openly the subset measures that govern their function's contribution to BET, TM, and BEAR. The map exposes each function's weaknesses insofar as each function's performance is clearly measurable against its own pre-dictions—predictions upon which important project decisions were based. Again, if there is going to be open sharing of data, the Return Map should not be used to penalize people for their forecasts. The race to market is a concerted effort that requires enthusiasm, not fear and apprehension. The judgments of the marketplace are generally all the correction a talented team requires.

The Return Map provides a visible superordinate goal for all the functions of the team and, in graphically repre-senting the common task, helps them collaborate. No graph can substitute for judgment and experience—yet there is no substitute either for basing judgment on an accurate picture of experience.

Originally published in January–February 1991
Reprint 91106

Knowing When to Pull the Plug

BARRY M. STAW AND JERRY ROSS

Executive Summary

WHO HASN'T PLAYED A GAME of poker when the chances of drawing an inside straight were slim and yet paid more money to see another card? Why, under equally chancy circumstances, do managers faced with a project that isn't going well, where the losses have already exceeded the estimates, plop down more money on the table to play another round? For lots of reasons, say the authors of this article. Some are psychological—we've been rewarded in the past for sticking to our guns, so why shouldn't the same thing happen this time? Some are social—no one likes a loser. And some are structural—important members of an organization are publicly committed.

Regardless of what combination of factors is at play, managers often take projects well past the point where they should have dropped them. How can organizations

65

end the gambling? Managers have to look closely at themselves and recognize which of the influences they may be under. The authors provide some probing questions to help. The rest of the job belongs to top management. Its course is to rethink what behavior it rewards and how it staffs projects and to ensure that its information systems report the real odds.

LAST YEAR YOU AUTHORIZED the expenditure of $500,000 for what you thought was a promising new project for the company. So far, the results have been disappointing. The people running the project say that with an additional $300,000 they can turn things around. Without extra funding, they cry, there is little hope. Do you spend the extra money and risk further losses, or do you cut off the project and accept the half-million-dollar write-off?

Managers face such quandaries daily. They range from developing and placing employees to choosing plant sites and making important strategic moves. Additional investment could either remedy the situation or lead to greater loss. In many situations, a decision to persevere only escalates the risks, and good management consists of knowing when to pull the plug.

These escalation situations are trouble. Most of us can think of times when we should have bailed out of a course of action. The Lockheed L 1011 fiasco and the Washington Public Supply System debacle (commonly referred to as WHOOPS) are spectacular examples of organizational failure to do so. Decisions to persist with these crippled ventures caused enormous losses.

Of course, all managers will make some mistakes and stick with some decisions longer than they ought to. Recent research has shown, however, that the tendency to pursue a failing course of action is not a random thing. Indeed, at times some managers, and even entire organizations, seem almost programmed to follow a dying cause.

What leads executives to act so foolishly? Are they people who should never have been selected for responsible positions? Are these organizations simply inept? Or are they generally competent managers and companies that find themselves drawn into decisional quicksand, with many forces driving them deeper? Though we think this last description is probably the right one, we don't think the tendency is uncheckable. Managers and organizations that often fall into escalation traps can take steps to avoid them.

Why Projects Go Out of Control

As a start to understanding why people get locked into losing courses of action, let's look first at what a purely rational decision-making approach would be. Consider, for example, the decision to pursue or scuttle an R&D or a marketing project. On the basis of future prospects, you'd have made the initial decision to pursue the project, and enough time would have passed to see how things were going. Ideally, you'd then reassess the situation and decide on future action. If you were following a fully rational approach, whatever losses might have occurred before this decision point would be irrelevant for your reassessment. With a cold, clear eye, you'd view the prospects for the future as well as your available options. Would the company be better off if it got out, continued with the project, or decided to invest more resources in it? You'd treat any previous expenses or losses as sunk costs, things that had happened in the past, not to be considered when you viewed the future.

In theory, pure rationality is great, but how many managers and organizations actually follow it? Not many. Instead, several factors encourage decision makers to become locked into losing courses of action.

The Project Itself

The first set of factors have to do with the project itself. "Is the project not doing well because we omitted an important factor from our calculations, or are we simply experiencing the downside of problems that we knew could occur?" "Are the problems temporary 'bad weather or a soon-to-be-settled supplier strike' or more permanent 'a steep downturn in demand'?" Expected or short-term problems are likely to encourage you to continue a project. You may even view them as necessary costs or investments for achieving large, long-term gains. If you expect problems to arise, when they do, they may convince you that things are going as planned.

A project's salvage value and closing costs can also impede withdrawal. An executive could simply terminate an ineffective advertising campaign in midstream, but stopping work on a half-completed facility is another story. A project that has very little salvage value and high closing costs—payments to terminated employees, penalties for breached contracts, and losses from the closing of facilities—will be much more difficult to abandon than a project in which expenditures are recoverable and exit is easy. It's understandable why so many financially questionable construction projects are pursued beyond what seems to be a rational point of withdrawal.

Consider the Deep Tunnel project in Chicago, a plan to make a major addition to the city's sewer system that will eventually improve its capacity to handle major storms. Although the project has absorbed millions of dollars, it won't deliver any benefits until the entire new system is completed. Unfortunately, as each year passes, the expected date of completion recedes into the future while the bill for work to be finished grows exponentially. Of course, no one would have advocated the project if the true costs had been known at the outset. Yet, once begun, few have argued to kill the project.

The problem is that the project was structured in ways that ensured commitment. First, the project managers viewed each setback as a temporary situation that was correctable over time with more money. Second, they perceived all moneys spent as investments toward a large payoff they'd reap when the project was complete. Third, expenditures were irretrievable: the laid pipe in the ground has no value unless the entire project is completed, and it would probably cost more to take the pipe out of the ground than it's worth. Thus, like many other large construction and R&D projects, investors in the Deep Tunnel have been trapped in the course of action. Even though what they receive in the end may not measure up to the cost of attaining it, they have to hang on until the end if they hope to recoup any of their investment.

Managers' Motivations

Most of the factors concerning projects that discourage hanging on are evident to managers. They may not fully factor closing costs and salvage value into their initial decisions to pursue certain courses of action (since new ventures are supposed to succeed rather than fail), but when deciding whether to continue a project or not, executives are usually aware of these factors. Less obvious to managers, however, are the psychological factors that influence the way information about courses of action are gathered, interpreted, and acted on.

We are all familiar with the idea that people tend to repeat behavior if they are rewarded and to stop it if they are punished. According to the theory of reinforcement, managers will withdraw from a course of action in the face of bad news. This interpretation, however, ignores people's history of rewards. Managers have often been rewarded for ignoring short-run disaster, for sticking it out through tough times. Successful executives—people whose decisions have turned out to be winners even when the outlook had appeared grim—are particularly susceptible. It's tough for managers with good track records to recognize that a certain course isn't a satisfactory risk, that things aren't once again going to turn their way.

Reinforcement theory also tells us that when people receive rewards intermittently (as from slot machines), they can become quite persistent. If a decline in rewards has been slow and irregular, a person can go on and on even after the rewards have disappeared. Unfortunately, many business situations that escalate to disaster involve precisely this type of reinforcement pattern. Sales may fall slowly in fits and starts, all the while offering enough hope that things will eventually return to normal. The hope makes it difficult to see that the market may have changed in fundamental ways. Revenues that slowly sour or costs that creep upward are just the kind of pattern that can cause managers to hang on beyond an economically rational point.

Research has also shown other reasons that executives fail to recognize when a project is beyond hope. People have an almost uncanny ability to see only what accords with their beliefs. Much like sports fans who concentrate on their own team's great plays and the other team's fouls, managers tend to see only what confirms their preferences. For example, an executive who is convinced that a project will be profitable will probably slant estimates of sales and costs to support the view. If the facts challenge this opinion, the manager may work hard to find reasons to discredit the source of information or the quality of the data. And if the data are ambiguous, the manager may seize on just those facts that support the opinion. Thus information biasing can be a major roadblock to sensible withdrawal from losing courses of action.

In addition to the effects of rewards and biased information, a third psychological mechanism may be at work. Sometimes even when managers recognize that they have suffered losses, they may choose to invest further resources in a project rather than accept failure. What may be fostering escalation in these cases is a need for self-justification. Managers may interpret bad news about a project as a personal failure. And, like most of us who are protective of our self-esteem, managers may hang on or even invest further resources to "prove" the project a success.

A number of experiments have verified this effect of self-justification. Those who are responsible for previous losses, for example, have generally been found to view projects more positively and to be more likely to commit additional resources to them than are people who have taken over projects in midstream. Managers who are not responsible for previous losses are less likely to "throw good money after bad" since they have less reason to justify previous mistakes.

Reinforcement, information biasing, and self-justification—three psychological factors that we're all subject to—can keep us committed to projects or actions we have started. Most managerial decisions, however, involve some additional factors that come into play when other people are around to observe our actions. These are social determinants.

Social Pressures

Managers may persist in a project not only because they don't want to admit error to themselves but also because they don't wish to expose their mistakes to others. No one wants to appear incompetent. Though persistence may be irrational from the organization's point of view, from the point of view of the beleaguered manager seeking to justify past behavior, it can be quite understandable. When a person's fate is tied to demands for performance and when accepting failure means loss of power or loss of a job, hanging on in the face of losses makes sense. Research has shown, for example, that job insecurity and lack of managerial support only heighten the need for external justification. Thus when a manager becomes closely identified with a project ("that's Jim's baby"), he can be essentially forced to defend the venture despite mounting losses and doubts about its feasibility.

Beyond the personal risks of accepting losses, our ideas of how a leader should act can also foster foolish persistence. Culturally, we associate persistence—"staying the course," "sticking to your guns," and "weathering the storm"—with strong leadership. Persistence that happens to turn out successfully is especially rewarded. For example, when we think about the people who have become heroes in business and politics (Iacocca and Churchill, for examples), we see leaders who have faced difficult and apparently failing situations but who have hung tough until they were successful. If people see persistence as a sign of leadership and withdrawal as a sign of weakness, why would they expect managers to back off from losing courses of action? Recent research demonstrates that even though it may not add to the welfare of the organization, persistence does make a manager look like a leader.

In short, the need to justify one's actions to others and to appear strong as a leader can combine with the three psychological factors to push managers into staying with a decision too long. This combination of forces does not, however, account for all debacles in which organizations suffer enormous losses through excessive commitment. In many of these cases structural factors also play a role.

Organizational Pushes and Pulls

Probably the simplest element impeding withdrawal from losing projects is administrative inertia. Just as individuals do not always act on their beliefs, organizations do not always base their practices on their preferences. All the rules, procedures, and routines of an organization as well as the sheer trouble it takes for managers to give up day-to-day activities in favor of a serious operational disruption can cause administrative inertia. Dropping a line of business may mean changing corporate layoff policies, and moving people to other projects may violate seniority and hiring procedures. Sometimes it's just easier not to rock the boat.

Beyond such simple inertia, the politics of a situation can prevent a bailout. British Columbia's decision to stage the world's fair Expo '86 is one of the most recent public examples of the power of political forces to sustain a costly course of action. Expo '86 was supposed to operate close to the financial break-even point. But as plans for the fair got under way, the expected losses burgeoned. At first, the planners tried to minimize the financial hazards by providing heartening but biased estimates of revenues and costs. When they finally accepted the more dire financial projections, however, and even the director recommended cancellation, the planners still went ahead with the fair. Politically it was too late: the fortunes of too many businesses in the province were tied to Expo, it was popular with the voters, and the future of the premier and his political party were aligned with it. The province created a lottery to cope with the expected $300 million deficit, and the fair opened as scheduled.

Though the Expo example comes from the public sector, political force may also sustain costly business projects. As a venture withers, not only those directly involved with it may work to maintain it, but other interdependent or politically aligned units may support it as well. If the project's advocates sit on governing bodies or budget committees, efforts to stop it will meet further resistance. If a review finally does occur, the estimates of the costs and benefits of continuing the venture will very likely be biased.

On occasion, support for a project can go even deeper than administrative inertia and politics. When a project

such as a long-standing line of business is closely identified with a company, to consider its discontinuation is to
consider killing the very purpose of the company. (Imagine Hershey without chocolate bars or Kimberly-Clark
without Kleenex.) A project or a division can become
institutionalized in an organization.

Consider the plight of Lockheed with its L 1011 Tri-
Star Jet program. Although every outside analysis of the
program found the venture unlikely to earn a profit,
Lockheed persisted with it for more than a decade and
accumulated enormous losses. The problem was not
ending the project per se but what it symbolized. The L
1011 was Lockheed's major entry in the commercial avia-
tion market (in which it had been a pioneer), and Lockheed shrank from being identified as simply a defense
contractor.

Pan American World Airways has recently gone
through a similar institutional process. More than most
airlines, Pan Am suffered huge losses after deregulation
of the industry; it was even in danger of not meeting its
debt obligations. Although the prospects for large profits
in the airline industry were dim, Pan Am chose to sell off
most of its other more profitable assets—first the Pan
Am building in New York and then the Intercontinental
Hotels Corporation—so as to remain in its core business.
Finally, as losses continued, Pan Am sold its valuable
Pacific routes to United Air Lines. Following these
divestitures, the company was left with only U.S. and
international routes in corridors where competition is
heavy. Apparently, management didn't seriously consider the possibility of selling or closing the airline and
keeping most of the other profitable subsidiaries. Pan
Am is, after all, in the airline and not the real estate or
hotel business.

Not all the forces we've described are relevant to every case, and not all are of equal influence in the situations where they operate. In many instances, commitment to a course of action builds slowly. Psychological and social forces come into play first, and only later does the structure make its impact. And, in a few cases, because the rational point of withdrawal has long passed, even the economic aspects of a project can cry out for continuation.

Still, some executives do manage to get themselves and entire organizations out of escalating situations. There are solutions.

Steps Executives Can Take Themselves

Executives can do many things to prevent becoming overcommitted to a course of action. Some of these solutions they can take care of on their own. Others involve getting the organization to do things differently. Let's look first at the remedies that executives themselves can apply.

RECOGNIZE OVERCOMMITMENT

The most important thing for managers to realize is that they may be biased toward escalation. For all the reasons we have mentioned, executives may delude themselves into thinking that a project will pull through—that success is around the corner. Recognizing overcommitment is, however, easier to preach than to practice. It usually takes enthusiasm, effort, and even passion to get projects off the ground and running in bureaucratic organizations. The organization depends on these responses for vitality. Consequently, the line between an optimistic, can-do attitude and overcommitment is very thin and often difficult to distinguish.

SEE ESCALATION FOR WHAT IT IS

How, then, can managers know whether they have crossed the threshold between the determination to get things done and overcommitment? Although the distinction is often subtle, they can clarify matters by asking themselves the following questions.

1. Do I have trouble defining what would constitute failure for this project or decision? Is my definition of failure ambiguous, or does it shift as the project evolves?

2. Would failure on this project radically change the way I think of myself as a manager or as a person? Have I bet the ranch on this venture for my career or for my own satisfaction?

3. Do I have trouble hearing other people's concerns about the project, and do I sometimes evaluate others' competence on the basis of their support for the project?

4. Do I generally evaluate how various events and actions will affect the project before I think about how they'll affect other areas of the organization or the company as a whole?

5. Do I sometimes feel that if this project ends, there will be no tomorrow?

If a manager has answered yes to one or more of these questions, the person is probably overcommitted to a project.

BACK OFF

Just knowing that one is under the sway of escalation can help. But knowing is not enough. It is also necessary to take some steps to avoid over-commitment. One way is to schedule regular times to step back and look at a project from an outsider's perspective. A good question to ask oneself at these times is, "If I took over this job for the first time today and found this project going on, would I support it or get rid of it?" Managers could take their cues from bankers. When they take over others' portfolios, bankers usually try to clean up any troubled loans since they want to maximize the future returns associated with their own loan activity. Managers can also encourage their subordinates to reevaluate decisions. Most critical here is establishing a climate in which, regardless of whether the data are supportive or critical of the ongoing project, people convey accurate information. Just stating a "nothing but the truth" policy, however, is usually not enough to change the pattern of information reporting. The messenger with extremely critical but important information needs an explicit reward.

One forum for getting objective and candid feedback is a variant of the currently popular quality circle. Managers could regularly convene key staff members for "decision circles," in which fellow employees would offer honest evaluations of the hurdles a project faces and its prospects. Managers from other departments or sections might also attend or even chair such sessions to ensure an objective look at the problems. Managers might also hold regular "exchanges of perspective" in which colleagues could help each other see the truth about their operations.

Change the Organization

Though it is possible to come up with an array of decision aids to help managers gain an objective perspective about the projects they run, one could argue that the problem of escalation is larger than any one person, that it's organizational in scope. Unfortunately, such a pessimistic view is at least partially correct. Much of what causes escalation is in the nature of organizations, not people.

If organizational action is called for, what can the system do to minimize escalation?

TURN OVER ADMINISTRATORS

One way to reduce the commitment to a losing course of action is to replace those associated with the original policy or project. If overcommitment stems from psychological and social forces facing the originators of the action, then their removal eliminates some of the sources of commitment.

Turning over project managers can of course be both disruptive and costly. Moreover, because people who were once associated with the discontinued venture may still be committed to it, management may find it difficult to draw the appropriate line for making a purge. Nonetheless, to make a clean break with the past, many organizations do make occasional personnel sweeps, sometimes more for their symbolic value than because of any real differences in decision making.

Still, we don't recommend turnover as the way to make changes. Like treating the disease by killing the patient, taking committed decision makers off a project may produce nothing but a demoralized staff and disaffected managers hesitant to try again.

SEPARATE DECISION MAKERS

One technique for reducing commitment that is far less drastic than turnover is to separate initial from subsequent decisions concerning a course of action. In some banks, for example, a "workout group" handles problem loans rather than the people who originally funded and serviced the loans. The idea is not only that specialists should be involved in recouping bank funds but also that these officers are able to handle the loans in a more objective way than those who made the first decisions about the accounts. Industrial companies could also make use of such procedures. They could separate funding from new-product-development decisions and hiring from promotion decisions. They could keep deliberations on whether to discontinue lines of business apart from day-to-day management decisions.

REDUCE THE RISK OF FAILURE

Another way to reduce commitment is to lessen the risk of failure. Because project failure can spell the end to an otherwise promising career, an administrator may be forced to defend a losing course of action. In a no-win dilemma, the trapped manager may think, "Things look bleak now, but there's no point in my suggesting that the company withdraw. If the project doesn't succeed, I have no future here anyway."

In some companies, management has reduced the costs of failure by providing rationalizations for losing courses of action and excuses for their managers. People are told that the losses are beyond anyone's control or that the fault lies with more general economic conditions, government regulation, or foreign competition. Although this route takes managers off the hook, it doesn't help them see a losing course for what it is or how they may avoid making the mistakes again.

Most companies do not want to take the pressure off their managers to perform as winners. Yet because a strong fear of failure can cause over-commitment, management is better off setting only a moderate cost for failure, something to avoid but not to fear intensely. A large computer company, for example, puts managers who have made big mistakes in a "penalty box." It makes them ineligible for major assignments for up to a year. After the penalty period, the managers are restored to full status in the organization and are again eligible to run major projects. Organizations trying to cope with escalation situations may find such a compromise between support for failure and demand for competence helpful.

IMPROVE THE INFORMATION SYSTEM

Several laboratory experiments have shown that people will withdraw from escalating situations when they see the high costs of persisting. The presentation of such negative data is more difficult in organizations, however. Because no one wants to be the conveyer of bad news, information is filtered as it goes up the hierarchy. Furthermore, because those intimately involved with a project are not likely to distribute unflattering and less-than-optimistic forecasts, information is also biased at the source.

What, then, can organizations do to improve their information reporting? The most common solution is to increase their use of outside experts and consultants. The problem with consultants, however, is that they are no more likely to hear the truth than anyone else in the organization, and they also may not find it easy to tell management what it doesn't want to hear.

A better solution is to try to improve the honesty of reporting throughout the organization. By rewarding process as highly as product, managers can encourage candid reporting. The purpose of rewarding managers for the way a process is carried out is to make them attend as much to the quality of analysis and decision making as to the final results. Instead of acting as champions who inflate the prospects of their own projects and minimize their risks, managers offered process rewards are motivated to recognize problems and deal with them.

At the outset of projects, companies should encourage the creation of fail-safe options, ways to segment projects into small, achievable parts, and analyses of the costs of withdrawal. Later in the life of projects, companies should reward honest recognition of problems and clear examination of the alternatives, including withdrawal.

This kind of reward system is quite different from the usual practice of giving people recognition for success on their projects and punishing them for failure on their undertakings. Yet it is a system that should reduce many of the forces for escalation.

Boosting Experimentation

As we noted earlier in our discussion, an entire organization can be so caught up in supporting a project—especially an institutionalized one—that it ignores the cost of persistence.

Rather than trying to discredit an institutionalized project on economic grounds, a good strategy for withdrawal from it is to reduce its links with the central purposes of the organization. A useful tactic is to label the project peripheral or experimental so that managers can treat it on its own merits rather than as a symbol of the organization's central goal or mission.

Ideally, managers should consider all ventures imperfect and subject to question in an "experimenting organization." Every program should be subject to regular reconsideration (á la zero-based budgeting), and every line of business should be for sale at the right price. In such an experimenting organization, projects wouldn't become institutionalized to the point where management couldn't judge them on their own costs and benefits. And because managers in such a system would be judged as much for recognition of problems facing their units and how they cope with them as for success and failure, experimenting organizations should be extremely flexible. When a market or a technology changes, the experimenting organization would not simply try to patch up the old product or plant but would be quick to see when it is best to pull the plug and start anew.

References

1. For more complete reviews of escalation research, see Barry M. Staw and Jerry Ross, "Understanding Escalation Situations: Antecedents, Prototypes, and Solutions," in *Research in Organizational Behavior*, ed. L.L. Cummings and Barry M. Staw (Greenwich, CT: JAI Press, 1987); and Joel Brockner and Jeffrey Z. Rubin, *Entrapment in Escalating Conflicts* (New York: Springer-Verlag, 1985).

2. See Gregory B. Northcraft and Gerrit Wolf, "Dollars, Sense, and Sunk Costs: A Lifecycle Model of Resource Allocation," *Academy of Management Review*, April 1984, p. 22.

3. For experiment results, see Barry M. Staw, "Knee-deep in the Big Muddy: A Study of Escalating Commitment to a Chosen Course of Action," in *Organizational Behavior and Human Performance*, June 1976, p. 27; Alan Tegar, *Too*

Much Invested to Quit (New York: Pergamon Press, 1980); Max H. Bazerman, R.I. Beekum, and F. David Schoorman, "Performance Evalution in a Dynamic Context: A Laboratory Study of the Impact of Prior Commitment to the Ratee," *Journal of Applied Psychology*, December 1982, p. 873.

4. Frederick V. Fox and Barry M. Staw, "The Trapped Administrator: The Effects of Job Insecurity and Policy Resistance upon Commitment to a Course of Action," *Administrative Science Quarterly*, September 1979, p. 449.

5. Barry M. Staw and Jerry Ross, "Commitment in an Experimenting Society: An Experiment on the Attribution of Leadership from Administrative Scenarios," *Journal of Applied Psychology*, June 1980, p. 249.

6. See Roy J. Lewicki, "Bad Loan Psychology: Entrapment and Commitment in Financial Lending," Graduate School of Business Administration Working Paper No. 80-25 (Durham, NC: Duke University, 1980).

7. Bruce E. McCain, "Continuing Investment Under Conditions of Failure: A Laboratory Study of the Limits to Escalation," *Journal of Applied Psychology*, May 1986, p. 280; and Edward G. Conlon and Gerrit Wolf, "The Moderating Effects of Strategy, Visibility, and Involvement on Allocation Behavior: An Extension of Staw's Escalation Paradigm," *Organizational Behavior and Human Performance*, October 1980, p. 172.

8. Donald T. Campbell, "Reforms as Experiments," *American Psychologist*, April 1969, p. 409.

Originally published in March–April 1987
Reprint 87212

Why Bad Projects Are So Hard to Kill

ISABELLE ROYER

Executive Summary

EVEN AT THE PROTOTYPE STAGE, experts were saying the technology was obsolete. Yet, in the face of tepid consumer response, the company stubbornly kept increasing production capacity and developing new models. By the time it was finally killed, the initiative had cost the company an astounding $580 million and had tied up resources for 14 years.

The product was RCA's SelectaVision videodisc recorder, and its story is hardly unique. Companies make similar mistakes—if on a somewhat smaller scale—all the time.

But why? No one comes to work saying, "I'm going to pursue a project that will waste my company millions of dollars." Quite the opposite. They come to work full of excitement about a project they believe in. And that, sur- prisingly, can be the root of all the trouble—a fervent belief in the inevitability of a project's ultimate success. Starting, naturally enough, with a project's champion, this faith can spread throughout the organization, leading everyone to believe collectively in the product's viability and to view any signs of impending doom merely as temporary setbacks.

This phenomenon is documented here in two chillingly detailed case studies, one involving Essilor, the world's largest maker of corrective lenses for eyeglasses, and the other involving Lafarge, the largest producer of building materials. By counterexample, they point the way toward avoiding such morasses: assembling project teams not entirely composed of like-minded people and putting in place—and sticking to—well-defined review processes. Both cases also show that if it takes a project champion to get a project up and running, it may take a new kind of organizational player—an "exit champion"— to push an irrationally exuberant organization to admit when enough is enough.

Y OU CAN STILL FIND THEM on eBay, sleek and gleaming videodisc players with LP-sized discs. The product: RCA's SelectaVision—one of the biggest consumer electronics flops of all time.

But it isn't simply the monumental failure in the marketplace that makes the SelectaVision story worth remembering. It's that RCA insisted on plowing money into the product long after all signs pointed to near certain failure. When the company developed its first prototype in 1970, some experts already considered the phonograph-like technology obsolete. Seven years later, with the quality of VCRs improving and digital technology on the horizon, every one of RCA's competitors had abandoned videodisc research. Even in the face of tepid consumer response to SelectaVision's launch in 1981, RCA continued to develop new models and invest in production capacity. When the product was finally killed in 1984, it had cost the company an astounding $580 million and had tied up resources for 14 years.

Companies make similar mistakes—if on a somewhat more modest scale—all the time. Of course, hindsight is 20/20; it's easy after the fact to criticize bold bets that didn't pay off. But too often managers charge ahead in the face of mounting evidence that success is pretty well unachievable.

Why can't companies kill projects that are clearly doomed? Is it just poor management? Bureaucratic inertia? My research has uncovered something quite different. Hardly the product of managerial incompetence or entrenched bureaucracy, the failures I've examined resulted, ironically, from a fervent and widespread belief among managers in the inevitability of their projects' ultimate success. This sentiment typically originates, naturally enough, with a project's champion; it then spreads throughout the organization, often to the highest levels, reinforcing itself each step of the way. The result is what I call collective belief, and it can lead an otherwise rational organization into some very irrational behavior.

Of course, a strongly held conviction and the refusal to let inevitable setbacks undermine it are just what you need to get a project up and running. But there is a dark side: As the project moves forward, faith can blind you to increasingly negative feedback—from the lab, from vendors and partners, from customers.

To better understand why this happens and what can be done to prevent it, I analyzed two failed product innovations at two large French companies. (For a brief

description of my research, see "What Were They Thinking?" at the end of this article.) One was a new lens created by Essilor, the world's largest maker of corrective
lenses for eyeglasses. The other was an industrial additive used in manufacturing paper, paint, and plastics,
developed by Lafarge, the largest producer of building
materials. In both cases, the projects absorbed millions
of dollars of investment before the companies finally
abandoned them.

My analysis revealed a number of practices that can
help companies avoid this kind of disaster. For one, they
can assemble project teams not entirely composed of people enthusiastically singing from the same hymnbook.
They can put in place a well-defined review process—and
then follow it. Perhaps most important, companies need
to recognize the role of "exit champions": managers with
the temperament and credibility to question the prevail-
ing belief, demand hard data on the viability of the project, and, if necessary, forcefully make the case that it
should be killed. While the importance of project champions is well documented, the value of someone who is able
to pull the plug on a project before it becomes a money
sink hasn't generally been appreciated.

Faith That Wouldn't Be Shattered

Essilor has long been proud of its research. In 1959, it
invented the Varilux "progressive" lens, for instance,
which corrects both near- and farsightedness without
the telltale lines that denote traditional bifocals. But this
story starts in the summer of 1979, when a similar breakthrough appears possible. Since 1974, the company has
been working on a composite glass-and-plastic material
that's lightweight, shatter resistant, scratch resistant,

and light sensitive. Now a researcher has come up with a way to make a lens from this material. Essilor's research manager immediately takes a personal interest in the idea, and he orders the creation of a trial lens. Two days later, it's done.

The news spreads quickly throughout the company and is greeted enthusiastically. The research manager seeks and gets approval to proceed with additional research. The CEO himself helps select the managers who will oversee the project, many of whom have worked together on the Varilux lens and other successful projects.

Early on, some questions are raised about the potential cost of this new composite lens, as well as its durability. It's common for layers of any composite material to separate. Indeed, the director of research and manufacturing questions whether the product is even viable. But his concern isn't heeded because he is, as one colleague says, "always skeptical." No initial marketing studies are conducted, but none had been done for Varilux, either; in both cases, the projects are driven by the exciting technology. Based on the current sales of other Essilor products, internal estimates predict sales of nearly 40 million units a year by 1985. In April 1980, the project is accepted for development and a target launch date is set for late 1981. Excitement is high.

In September 1980 though, some bad news arrives: Corning, which supplies the glass for the composite lens, says that meeting the U.S. Food and Drug Administration's test for shatter resistance is proving more difficult than expected. If this continues to be the case, company estimates indicate that sales in 1985 will total just 10 million units. Then, pilot tests in January 1981 reveal a number of other problems, including a tendency of the lens to crack as it's mounted into the frame. Researchers are confident that this problem can be solved (though the company later decides it will offer an exchange guarantee to opticians). Despite the problems revealed in the pilot test, production facilities are built, and trial manufacturing begins. But now another issue arises: Production costs turn out to be twice what was forecast, which will make the lens as much as six times as expensive as normal lenses.

Essilor proudly launches the lens in June 1982. The president of the company sends a sample to the French Ministry of Industry. One researcher tucks a prototype away in his attic so that he can someday show his son "how you do innovation." The manager who unveils the lens at a press conference says he feels a sense of "real jubilation."

Customers are less enthusiastic: Opticians complain about the price and the difficulties of mounting the lens. Essilor has forecast sales of 200,000 units by the end of 1982, a number limited solely by initial production capacity. But sales reach just 20,000 by that date. What's more, concerns about the tendency of the lens's layers to separate are proving justified.

These setbacks are an emotional blow to those involved in the project but are not enough to destroy their belief. "It felt like a knockout," one recalls. "Still, although we were in shock, we knew failure was impossible." After all, those involved point out, initial sales of Varilux had also been slow, because people found the progressive lens difficult to get used to.

The problems continue. In 1985, Essilor launches a second-generation lens meant to fix the separation problems, but it fails to do so. Sales drop below 15,000 units a year. In 1986, a modified composite material solves the separation problem, but the lens remains difficult for opticians to mount in the frame. Researchers are asked to fix this problem before the company will commit itself to launching a third-generation lens.

After a year of further research, the problem still isn't solved. But the research manager argues to the executive committee that, since the separation problem has been corrected, the third-generation lens should be launched. The company does so at the end of 1987, and, in 1988, sales grow to a lackluster 50,000 units.

Then, in the spring of 1989, because of retirements and a restructuring of the company's overall research and production activities, four new managers join the project. A new research manager replaces the lens's foremost champion. In September, the new research manager completes his own evaluation of the project. Sales are still low, and the U.S. market remains out of reach because the lens still hasn't passed the FDA test. The investment needed to develop a full range of products, including a progressive lens, could double what has been spent so far. He recommends that the lens be abandoned.

Top management rejects his recommendation. The company does decide, however, to conduct a thorough evaluation of the project. To no one's surprise, a business analysis shows that the lens currently doesn't generate a profit. But a marketing study further concludes that even if the quality problems are ironed out, potential sales will reach only 1.5 million units per year, a fraction of the 40 million originally predicted. The implication: The lens will never be very profitable.

In September 1990, with quality problems still unsolved and no prospect of passing the FDA test, the company decides to call an immediate halt to research on the lens and stop production within a year. It's been ten years since the first warning signs arose. It has cost Essilor Fr 300 million, or more than $50 million in 1990 dollars.

A Belief in Crystals

Lafarge, like Essilor, has a big stake in the success of the product it is developing. It's early 1985, and research that Lafarge has done on the crystallization of gypsum, a mineral commonly used in the company's core building-materials businesses, looks like it is about to bear fruit. The engineering manager of the gypsum division has concluded that the crystals could serve as a superior substitute for the ground-up minerals commonly used in making paper and paint. The market could be large: One internal forecast puts potential annual sales at Fr 400 million, or about $40 million at the time. And pride as well as profit is at stake. Lafarge has typically grown through acquisition; here is a chance for the company to prove it can grow organically by leveraging its resources into new businesses.

Later that year, the engineering manager of the gypsum division begins research on the use of the crystals as a paper filler (something added to paper stock to improve such physical or optical properties as texture or opacity). He finds a partner in a big paper producer, Aussedat Rey. The engineering manager and his boss, the division's director of operations, seek and receive project backing from Lafarge's top management. Because the crystal-based approach is so innovative, enthusiasm quickly grows.

Over the next several years, the project enjoys both successes and setbacks. The paper filler product is superior in a number of ways to existing fillers, and the crystals turn out to have another potential application in plastics manufacturing. Aussedat Rey agrees to pay for further paper filler tests.

These highlight several problems. The product has the potential to clog certain papermaking machines. And it is not concentrated enough, making it relatively expensive for customers to use. Researchers are confident, however, that these problems can be solved. Lafarge's top management accepts the project for development, including applications for paper, paint, and plastics, and sets 1990 as the target launch date.

Aussedat Rey's first production trial of the paper filler in December 1987 is a technical success, although the paper company still wants a more concentrated version. The successful trial heightens Lafarge's optimism; informal estimates of annual sales grow to Fr 1 billion, or about $190 million in 1988 dollars. To be sure, projections indicate that the paper filler itself probably won't be profitable. But the full range of products for paper, paint, and plastics taken together should be. Unfortunately, only the paper filler has advanced beyond the laboratory stage.

Still, people are eager to get the product to market. To begin production in 1990, the gypsum division's director of operations needs funding to break ground on the plant in 1989. At the end of 1988, Lafarge's top management, aware that tests on the more-concentrated version of the paper filler have not yet been run, approves funding for the plant, so long as certain criteria are met. Before the money is released, the project team must have "verified the feasibility of the manufacturing process in the pilot workshop and the product's quality and acceptability to customers."

This tentative go-ahead is greeted enthusiastically by project members. A lone dissenting voice is Lafarge's new mineral-fillers manager, recently recruited from a consumer products company. He raises concerns about remaining technical challenges, especially after a more-concentrated version of the paper filler fails a new test at Aussedat Rey. But his concerns are generally ignored because of his lack of experience in industrial products. In fact, others involved in the project repeatedly remind him of this fact. He stops raising questions—and ultimately resigns.

Meanwhile, Aussedat Rey is showing less interest in the paper filler and repeatedly delays further trials. (It later will sever its relationship with Lafarge because the price of the paper filler is too high.) The paper filler's "quality and acceptability to customers"—the criteria that must be met to receive funding for the plant—seem far from assured. And yet, after a presentation by members of the project, top management gives the plant a green light, and it is inaugurated in September 1990. Several weeks later, at Lafarge's annual meeting of researchers from labs across the company, the paper filler researchers and their managers present the project as an example of a successful internal research initiative.

But the new plant remains idle, as no product has yet emerged from the lab that is ready for production and no customer or partner has been found to fund further tests.

Meanwhile, one of the project's champions, the gypsum division's director of operations, has left Lafarge for health reasons and has been replaced by an operations director from another division of the company. He forms a task force to formally evaluate the viability of the project. This isn't easy because of the lack of data. For example, although an initial market study was done, there have been no follow-ups to gauge demand for a product that is now likely to lack some of the features originally envisioned. Still, in April 1991, the task force's report confirms that the paper filler itself won't be profitable and estimates that two years and another Fr 30 million (about $5.3 million in 1991 dollars) would be needed to get other products ready for pilot testing. The new director of operations recommends terminating the project.

Most team members agree with the factual findings, but many reject the recommendation that the project be killed. So, although top management stops development of the paper filler, it authorizes continued research on products to be used in paper coating and plastics manufacturing. At the end of 1991, however, a test of the paper-coating product produces poor results and offers little hope that it can be improved. In early 1992, the plant is sold and the entire project is stopped, having cost a total of Fr 150 million (nearly $30 million in 1992 dollars) over seven years.

The Seductive Appeal of Collective Belief

So what got into the decision makers at these two companies? Why did Essilor persist with the development of its new lens in the face of so much negative evidence? Why did Lafarge build a brand-new production facility before determining whether its gypsum crystal additive had a future in the marketplace?

These were not cases of bureaucratic inertia. If anything, the procedures and controls over these projects were too lax rather than too unresponsive or inflexible. Nor were these cases in which project champions were flogging a dead horse to justify their original touting of it. What the many interviews and myriad contemporary documents reveal in both companies is the power, and troublesome implications, of a very human impulse: the desire to believe in something—in these situations, in the projects' ultimate success. In both companies, this belief was held not just by a handful of individuals but by much of their organizations.

How does that happen? Collective belief arises because individual belief is often contagious, particularly when it reinforces others' perceptions and desires. When this is the case, the belief can spread easily among the various decision makers who control a project's fate. Here's how that played out at Lafarge and Essilor.

THE EMERGENCE OF BELIEF

The original true believer is a project champion, who holds an unyielding conviction—based, often as not, on a hunch rather than on strong evidence—that a project will succeed. This belief then spreads to others; how quickly and with what intensity depends on a number of factors. Some of these are organizational and some are particular to the champion—for example, his personal credibility and charisma and the robustness and range of his social network within the company. Indeed, if the champion's reputation is strong enough, the belief can pass from person to person until it is shared by individuals who don't even know the champion and know little of the project. At Lafarge, two project members candidly admitted that they couldn't truly assess the potential of the new product but took the word of one of the project's champions that it was a winner.

Belief in a project is all the more contagious when its ultimate success is something that people greatly desire.

For both Essilor and Lafarge, the two projects furthered important companywide goals: the development of products that embodied a strong technological tradition of "research for the sake of vision" at Essilor, and the desire to generate organic growth rather than growth through acquisition at Lafarge.

But a project can also satisfy individual desires, ones that are often quite various and even potentially conflicting. Some at Essilor reported they saw the lens as something "that would permanently eliminate competitors." Others hoped the project would maintain employment levels in the glass factories as plastic lenses grew in popularity. Some senior executives saw the composite glass-and-plastic lens as a way to strengthen corporate culture: Essilor was born from the merger of Essel, a glass-lens manufacturer, and Silor, a rival that made plastic lenses, and the two divisions still competed against each other.

At Lafarge, some viewed the new additive as a way to enhance the reputation of the company's R&D function. Others saw it as a strategically important move beyond building materials. In both companies, the collective belief served as an umbrella that sheltered an array of hopes and dreams; those, in turn, worked together to reinforce the collective belief.

THE PERSISTENCE OF BELIEF

Once a collective belief takes hold, it tends to perpetuate itself. For one thing, groups have a way of drowning out dissent. At Essilor and Lafarge, both lone initial dissidents—Essilor's director of research and manufacturing and Lafarge's mineral-fillers manager—were generally ignored or told that the questions they raised reflected their lack of experience or competence. Eventually, they stopped raising questions. This self-censorship gave the groups an illusion of unanimity and invulnerability, which in turn helped sustain individual belief. One manager at Essilor said that the lens's failure in the market in 1982 raised doubts in his mind. But he chose not to voice these and, because of the group's apparent unanimity, soon forgot them.

Curiously, setbacks, rather than undermining faith, often drive people to work all the harder to maintain it. Despite the Essilor lens's poor market performance, the company continued to produce it in vast quantities, consistently more than were sold. Since project members believed the market failure was only a prelude to ultimate success, they exhibited what one manager called "technological relentlessness" in their pursuit of both improvements and customers.

This intensity is not surprising, given the emotional attachment people feel for a project they passionately believe in. As one Essilor manager said of an early version of the lens: "It was a dream, and a dream come true on top of that! The product existed! It was beautiful." Another manager, recalling a setback in lens development, observed, "We didn't dare wonder whether we should stop or not. It was too hard."

THE CONSEQUENCES OF BELIEF

The greatest danger posed by an organization's collective belief in a project is that problems, even if acknowledged, won't be seen as signs of failure—or at least as issues that should be resolved before moving on to the next stage of development. At Essilor, some managers explained away the lukewarm initial demand for the lens as an aberration related to the soon-to-be-solved technical problem of layer separation, forgetting that the market was generally unaware of this problem. At Lafarge, one manager knew that the decision to build the plant was probably premature, given the available test results for the product, but he said nothing because he was eager to move forward on an enterprise everyone was certain would succeed. Managers at both companies referred to the blindness that resulted from their faith in the projects.

This blindness persists in part because collective belief undermines normal organizational procedures and safeguards. For one thing, the enthusiasm generated by faith in a project can lead to an unrealistically tight development timetable. Essilor canceled some tests and substituted shorter, less reliable ones in order to stick to its aggressive development schedule. A test to see how durable the lenses remained over time, for example, was shortened from two years to six months. Lafarge's desire to remain on schedule was the driving force in the construction of the plant before necessary tests on the additive had been completed.

Enthusiasm also can result in lenient procedures for reviewing the viability of a product throughout its development. For instance, scratch-resistance specifications for Essilor's new lens were not defined until 1990, eight years after the product was initially launched. Furthermore, widespread enthusiasm can lead to the formation of a project team filled with, and overseen by, uncritical boosters of the initiative.

Together, these factors can create a reinforcing chain that perpetuates collective belief. Decision makers' faith in the project results in an absence of clear decision criteria, which leads to ambiguous information, which in turn favors wishful thinking by those decision makers and further bolsters their belief in the project's success. In a sense, the project takes on a life of its own.

Avoiding the Dangers of Blind Faith

In your own company, you have undoubtedly known projects that dragged on but went nowhere. You may be aware of a handful of bad projects that are grinding along, or even picking up speed, right now. How can companies prevent this sort of thing? How could the managers at Essilor, for example, have known that the composite lens project wouldn't turn out the way the Varilux lens effort did?

They probably couldn't, at least for a while. But they could have done a number of things that would have made them better able to judge their progress and counteract the distorting effects of collective belief. Two kinds of safeguards can be built into a project before it even gets under way. Another one requires a manager involved in a project to play an important, new role.

BEWARE OF CHEERLEADING SQUADS

All too often, project teams are self-selected. They include people who have volunteered because they share an initial enthusiasm for the project. They may even have worked together on successful projects in the past. They know the drill and can anticipate one another's moves. In fact, they know them too well. As they interact, there are none of the awkward missteps or misunderstandings that can produce unexpected insights—or signs of trouble. Warning flags that do appear may be ignored; after all, everyone is rooting for something they believe in.

Executives launching a project would do well, then, to include skeptics along with believers in the project teams from the outset, paying particular attention to those who will be directly involved in making decisions. Then, over the course of the initiative, some decision makers should be replaced with others, who will look at the project with fresh eyes.

At Essilor and Lafarge, top management populated the projects with true believers. In fact, in both cases, the sole initial critics joined the projects somewhat by chance. Essilor's director of research and manufacturing was involved only because he was the immediate supervisor of the manager of the plant where the lens would be made. Lafarge's mineral-fillers manager had originally been hired for another job and joined the project only because Lafarge had difficulty finding someone with both minerals and project expertise to fill out the team. At Essilor, personal relationships also came into play; some members had been friends for 20 years—a further reason that robust criticism, which might jeopardize those friendships, didn't emerge.

Only when turnover occurred for reasons unrelated to the project—retirement, health problems, the restructuring of a companywide research function—was the cohesiveness of the project groups disrupted and some measure of objectivity introduced.

ESTABLISH AN EARLY WARNING SYSTEM

From the start, no matter how exciting or important a project is, a company needs to make sure that its control procedures and criteria for evaluating project viability at each stage of development are truly working—that they are clearly defined, rigorous, and actually met. Big companies like Essilor and Lafarge typically have these kinds of effective internal controls for all sorts of processes— for example, "stage gates" that companies must go through as they proceed with a potential acquisition. But they can easily forget to establish such structures at the beginning of a project that seems bound for glory. Or even if they do establish processes for good decision making, they can end up ignoring them—or the results— amid the excitement generated by a new project.

Lafarge executives concede that they failed to adhere to their own decision criteria when they went ahead and built the plant—although the criteria were vague enough to make this fairly easy to do. Essilor had several clear procedures for testing the lens during development that weren't followed; others produced negative results, which were ignored. As one Essilor manager said: "The decision to launch was implicit. It was just a question of when."

RECOGNIZE THE ROLE OF THE EXIT CHAMPION

Sometimes it takes an individual, rather than growing evidence, to shake the collective belief of a project team. If the problem with unbridled enthusiasm starts as an unintended consequence of the legitimate work of a project champion, then what may be needed is a countervailing force—an exit champion. These people are more than devil's advocates. Instead of simply raising questions about a project, they seek objective evidence showing that problems in fact exist. This allows them to challenge—or, given the ambiguity of existing data, conceivably even to confirm—the viability of a project. They then take action based on the data. At both Essilor and Lafarge, exit champions—the new research manager at Essilor, and the new operations director at Lafarge—joined the projects as evidence of their unpromising futures was mounting. But supporters were still clinging to the shreds of positive evidence that occasionally emerged—or ignoring the evidence altogether. Had it not been for these exit champions, team members said later, the projects probably would have continued for months or even years.

To be effective, an exit champion needs to be directly involved in the project; a negative assessment from someone based elsewhere in the company is too easy to dismiss as ill-informed or motivated by organizational rivalry. The exit champion also needs a high degree of personal credibility. The managers at Essilor and Lafarge who had raised questions about the lens and paper filler during the early development stages lacked this credibility. Essilor's director of research and manufacturing was known within the organization as a naysayer; Lafarge's mineral-fillers manager, who came from another company, appeared to lack industry experience. The exit champions, by contrast, had been with their companies for a long time and were well regarded by top management. Both had a strong network of people at different levels of the company ready to provide support when they decided the project should be killed.

What kind of person would willingly assume such a role? Even if killing a project doesn't put an exit champion out of a job—the individuals at Essilor and Lafarge had responsibilities beyond the projects in question—the role, unlike that of a traditional project champion, seems to offer little in the way of prestige or other personal rewards. (For a discussion of the differences between the two roles, see "The Exit Champion and the Project Champion" at the end of this article.) In fact, the exit champion faces inevitable hostility from project supporters; those at Essilor and Lafarge were variously described as villains or dream breakers.

Consequently, exit champions need to be fearless, willing to put their reputations on the line and face the likelihood of exclusion from the camaraderie of the project team. They need to be determined: Both Essilor's and Lafarge's exit champions failed in their first attempts to stop their projects. Perhaps most important, exit champions need to have some incentive for putting themselves out to halt a bad project. For many, this will simply be an acute distaste for wasted effort. As one exit champion at another company I researched said, "When I work, I need to believe in what I do. I don't want to waste time on something that is worthless."

It is important to understand that an exit champion is not a henchman sent by top management to kill the project. The exit champions at Essilor and Lafarge certainly weren't: They were assigned their positions only because their predecessors had left the company, and they simply took the initiative to determine if their projects were likely to be successful. Indeed, it wasn't initially clear to either of them that their respective projects *should* be killed. Although signs that the projects wouldn't succeed were accumulating, in neither case was the evidence conclusive because it wasn't based on hard data.

Senior executives need to recognize the exit champion as a defined role that someone might play in the organization—otherwise, they may not know an exit champion for who he is and give him the support he will need. And they can take steps to create an environment in which such a savior would be more likely to emerge. Just as companies celebrate and recount stories of the great successes of product champions, they could perhaps identify and spread tales of courageous exit champions in their midst (or at other companies) who saved their organizations millions of dollars. Top managers should at the least make it clear that challenges to a popular project would be welcome or even rewarded. At the same time, though, they need to demand from the exit champion strong evidence of the project's weaknesses— just as they should have earlier demanded growing evidence of its viability.

It Couldn't Happen Here

When all is said and done, do Essilor's and Lafarge's experiences—not to mention RCA's in the case of its ill-fated SelectaVision—simply reflect bad business judgment? Were they nothing more nor less than dumb business moves? Aren't situations like these unlikely to be repeated at your company?

Don't bet on it. Although they may not always be played out on such a grand scale, stories like these are all too familiar in business. That's because belief is a powerful sentiment, and collective belief is even more powerful. Clearly, any project has to start with faith because there typically isn't much objective evidence, if any, at the beginning to justify it. But, as a project unfolds and investments increase, this faith has to be increasingly tested against the data. Indeed, the challenge for

managers in the "can-do" culture of business is to distinguish between belief as a key driver of success—and
belief as something that can blind managers to a project's ultimate failure.

What Were They Thinking?

HOW DO YOU GET AN accurate picture of an organization's belief in a project, especially after the fact? My
study of Essilor and Lafarge, which was conducted several years after the two projects analyzed in this article
were abandoned, lasted two years. It included several
dozen interviews with middle managers and senior executives involved in the projects. I also had access to a
range of company documents: reports, memos, written
notes, test results, marketing studies, business plans, and,
in each case, the analysis of an outside consultant.
Finally, for each company, I asked two executives—each
with a different view of the project—to review the lengthy
written summary of the project history I had prepared.

Researching events long after the fact can provide
perspective that would be absent from contemporary
research. But there is the danger that people's perceptions and conclusions will be colored because the project's outcome is known. To guard against this, all technical evaluations came from documents written during the
course of the project. In interviews, I asked people what
their opinions and feelings were at the time, not what
they thought now. Later, I cross-checked the interview
data with the written record. When there was a conflict, I
went back to the interviewees to ask for more details until
the data were consistent.

The Exit Champion and the Project Champion

AT BOTH ESSILOR AND LAFARGE, some of the projects' champions opposed the exit champions who successfully pulled the plugs on their projects. Although no public confrontations occurred in either case, the project champions raised with other project participants questions about the exit champions' intentions.

Such conflicts are interesting because in many ways the roles of the traditional project champion and the exit champion are similar. Just as innovations are unlikely to be implemented without champions, failing projects are unlikely to be halted without exit champions. In fact, the types of individuals who gravitate toward those roles are also similar.

Both project champions and exit champions must show initiative; after all, they have by definition assumed their roles rather than been assigned them. And they need to be energetic and determined enough to overcome the obstacles and inevitable skepticism they face. Given their similar personal traits, it's not surprising that, at a number of companies I studied, exit champions had been project champions at other points in their careers.

Differences between project champions and exit champions appear, however, in the particulars. For one thing, while project champions necessarily operate in an environment of uncertainty and ambiguity, exit champions need to remove ambiguity. They must gather hard data that will be convincing enough to overcome the opposition of believers. They need clear criteria for deciding whether to kill the project. When existing procedures don't include such criteria, they need to reach an agreement with believers on the criteria for assessing the new data; otherwise, reaching an agreement on the decision will be impossible. Thus, while project champions often violate procedures, exit champions typically have to introduce or restore them.

Project champions' reputations are often put at risk by their choice to champion what may turn out to be a failed project. Exit champions also put their reputations at risk, but the threat is of a different nature. Project champions run a long-term risk of being wrong—something that will become clear only if a project ultimately fails. Exit champions face the immediate risk that comes from challenging a popular project. That risk exists even if the exit champion is, in fact, ultimately right.

Originally published in February 2003
Reprint R0302C

How to Kill Creativity

TERESA M. AMABILE

Executive Summary

IN TODAY'S KNOWLEDGE ECONOMY, creativity is more important than ever. But many companies unwittingly employ managerial practices that kill it. How? By crushing their employees' *intrinsic motivation*—the strong internal desire to do something based on interests and passions.

Managers don't kill creativity on purpose. Yet in the pursuit of productivity, efficiency, and control—all worthy business imperatives—they undermine creativity. It doesn't have to be that way, says Teresa Amabile. Business imperatives can comfortably coexist with creativity. But managers will have to change their thinking first.

Specifically, managers will need to understand that creativity has three parts: expertise, the ability to think flexibly and imaginatively, and motivation. Managers can influence the first two, but doing so is costly and slow. It would be far more effective to increase employees' intrinsic motivation.

To that end, managers have five levers to pull: the amount of challenge they give employees, the degree of freedom they grant around process, the way they design work groups, the level of encouragement they give, and the nature of organizational support.

Take challenge as an example. Intrinsic motivation is high when employees feel challenged but not overwhelmed by their work. The task for managers, therefore, becomes matching people to the right assignments. Consider also freedom. Intrinsic motivation—and thus creativity—soars when managers let people decide *how* to achieve goals, not *what* goals to achieve.

Managers *can* make a difference when it comes to employee creativity. The result can be truly innovative companies in which creativity doesn't just survive but actually thrives.

WHEN I CONSIDER ALL the organizations I have studied and worked with over the past 22 years, there can be no doubt: creativity gets killed much more often than it gets supported. For the most part, this isn't because managers have a vendetta against creativity. On the contrary, most believe in the value of new and useful ideas. However, creativity is undermined unintentionally every day in work environments that were established— for entirely good reasons—to maximize business imperatives such as coordination, productivity, and control.

Managers cannot be expected to ignore business imperatives, of course. But in working toward these imperatives, they may be inadvertently designing organizations that systematically crush creativity. My research shows that it is possible to develop the best of both worlds: organizations in which business imperatives are attended to *and* creativity flourishes. Building such organizations, however, requires us to understand precisely what kinds of managerial practices foster creativity— and which kill it.

What Is Business Creativity?

We tend to associate creativity with the arts and to think of it as the expression of highly original ideas. Think of how Pablo Picasso reinvented the conventions of painting or how William Faulkner redefined fiction. In business, originality isn't enough. To be creative, an idea must also be appropriate—useful and actionable. It must somehow influence the way business gets done—by improving a product, for instance, or by opening up a new way to approach a process.

The associations made between creativity and artistic originality often lead to confusion about the appropriate place of creativity in business organizations. In seminars, I've asked managers if there is any place they *don't* want creativity in their companies. About 80% of the time, they answer, "Accounting." Creativity, they seem to believe, belongs just in marketing and R&D. But creativity can benefit every function of an organization. Think of activity-based accounting. It was an invention—an *accounting* invention—and its impact on business has been positive and profound.

Along with fearing creativity in the accounting department—or really, in any unit that involves systematic processes or legal regulations—many managers also hold a rather narrow view of the creative process. To them, creativity refers to the way people think—how inventively they approach problems, for instance. Indeed, thinking imaginatively is one part of creativity, but two others are also essential: *expertise* and *motivation*. See the exhibit "The Three Components of Creativity" for a visual representation.

Expertise encompasses everything that a person knows and can do in the broad domain of his or her work. Take, for example, a scientist at a pharmaceutical company who is charged with developing a blood-clotting drug for hemophiliacs. Her expertise includes her basic talent for thinking scientifically as well as all the knowledge and technical abilities that she has in the fields of medicine, chemistry, biology, and biochemistry.

The Three Components of Creativity

Within every individual, creativity is a function of three components: expertise, creative-thinking skills, and motivation. Can managers influence these components? The answer is an emphatic yes—for better or for worse—through workplace practices and conditions.

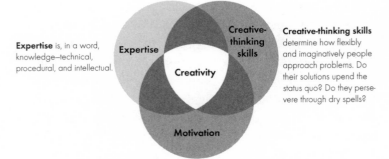

Expertise is, in a word, knowledge—technical, procedural, and intellectual.

Creative-thinking skills determine how flexibly and imaginatively people approach problems. Do their solutions upend the status quo? Do they persevere through dry spells?

Not all **motivation** is created equal. An inner passion to solve the problem at hand leads to solutions far more creative than do external rewards, such as money. This component—called *intrinsic motivation*—is the one that can be most immediately influenced by the work environment.

It doesn't matter how she acquired this expertise, whether through formal education, practical experience, or interaction with other professionals. Regardless, her expertise constitutes what the Nobel laureate, economist, and psychologist Herb Simon calls her "network of possible wanderings," the intellectual space that she uses to explore and solve problems. The larger this space, the better.

Creative thinking, as noted above, refers to *how* people approach problems and solutions—their capacity to put existing ideas together in new combinations. The skill itself depends quite a bit on personality as well as on how a person thinks and works. The pharmaceutical scientist, for example, will be more creative if her personality is such that she feels comfortable disagreeing with others—that is, if she naturally tries out solutions that depart from the status quo. Her creativity will be enhanced further if she habitually turns problems upside down and combines knowledge from seemingly disparate fields. For example, she might look to botany to help find solutions to the hemophilia problem, using lessons from the vascular systems of plants to spark insights about bleeding in humans.

As for work style, the scientist will be more likely to achieve creative success if she perseveres through a difficult problem. Indeed, plodding through long dry spells of tedious experimentation increases the probability of truly creative breakthroughs. So, too, does a work style that uses "incubation," the ability to set aside difficult problems temporarily, work on something else, and then return later with a fresh perspective.

Expertise and creative thinking are an individual's raw materials—his or her natural resources, if you will. But a third factor—motivation—determines what people will actually do. The scientist can have outstanding educational credentials and a great facility in generating new perspectives to old problems. But if she lacks the motivation to do a particular job, she simply won't do it; her expertise and creative thinking will either go untapped or be applied to something else.

My research has repeatedly demonstrated, however, that all forms of motivation do not have the same impact on creativity. In fact, it shows that there are two types of motivation—*extrinsic* and *intrinsic*, the latter being far more essential for creativity. But let's explore extrinsic first, because it is often at the root of creativity problems in business.

Extrinsic motivation comes from *outside* a person—whether the motivation is a carrot or a stick. If the scientist's boss promises to reward her financially should the blood-clotting project succeed, or if he threatens to fire her should it fail, she will certainly be motivated to find a solution. But this sort of motivation "makes" the scientist do her job in order to get something desirable or avoid something painful.

Obviously, the most common extrinsic motivator managers use is money, which doesn't necessarily stop people from being creative. But in many situations, it doesn't help either, especially when it leads people to feel that they are being bribed or controlled. More important, money by itself doesn't make employees passionate about their jobs. A cash reward can't magically prompt people to find their work interesting if in their hearts they feel it is dull.

But passion and interest—a person's internal desire to do something—are what intrinsic motivation is all about. For instance, the scientist in our example would be intrinsically motivated if her work on the blood-clotting drug was sparked by an intense interest in hemophilia, a personal sense of challenge, or a drive to crack a problem that no one else has been able to solve. When people are intrinsically motivated, they engage in their work for the challenge and enjoyment of it. The work *itself* is motivating. In fact, in our creativity research, my students, colleagues, and I have found so much evidence in favor of intrinsic motivation that we have articulated what we call the *Intrinsic Motivation Principle of Creativity*: people will be most creative when they feel motivated primarily by the interest, satisfaction, and challenge of the work itself—and not by external pressures. (For more on the differences between intrinsic and extrinsic motivation, see "The Creativity Maze" at the end of this article.)

Managing Creativity

Managers can influence all three components of creativity: expertise, creative-thinking skills, and motivation. But the fact is that the first two are more difficult and time consuming to influence than motivation. Yes, regular scientific seminars and professional conferences will undoubtedly add to the scientist's expertise in hemophilia and related fields. And training in brainstorming, problem solving, and so-called lateral thinking might give her some new tools to use in tackling the job. But the time and money involved in broadening her knowledge and expanding her creative-thinking skills would be great. By contrast, our research has shown that intrinsic motivation can be increased considerably by even subtle changes in an organization's environment. That is not to say that managers should give up on improving expertise and creative-thinking skills. But when it comes to pulling levers, they should know that those that affect intrinsic motivation will yield more immediate results.

More specifically, then, what managerial practices affect creativity? They fall into six general categories: challenge, freedom, resources, work-group features, supervisory encouragement, and organizational support. These categories have emerged from more than two decades of research focused primarily on one question: What are the links between work environment and creativity? We have used three methodologies: experiments, interviews, and surveys. While controlled experiments allowed us to identify causal links, the interviews and surveys gave us insight into the richness and complexity of creativity within business organizations. We have studied dozens of companies and, within those, hundreds of individuals and teams. In each research initiative, our goal has been to identify which managerial practices are definitively linked to positive creative outcomes and which are not.

For instance, in one project, we interviewed dozens of employees from a wide variety of companies and industries and asked them to describe in detail the most and least creative events in their careers. We then closely studied the transcripts of those interviews, noting the managerial practices—or other patterns—that appeared repeatedly in the successful creativity stories and, conversely, in those that were unsuccessful. Our research has also been bolstered by a quantitative survey instrument called KEYS. Taken by employees at any level of an organization, KEYS consists of 78 questions used to assess various workplace conditions, such as the level of support for creativity from top-level managers or the organization's approach to evaluation.

Taking the six categories that have emerged from our research in turn, let's explore what managers can do to enhance creativity—and what often happens instead. Again, it is important to note that creativity-killing practices are seldom the work of lone managers. Such practices usually are systemic—so widespread that they are rarely questioned.

CHALLENGE

Of all the things managers can do to stimulate creativity, perhaps the most efficacious is the deceptively simple task of matching people with the right assignments. Managers can match people with jobs that play to their expertise and their skills in creative thinking, *and* ignite intrinsic motivation. Perfect matches stretch employees' abilities. The amount of stretch, however, is crucial: not so little that they feel bored but not so much that they feel overwhelmed and threatened by a loss of control.

Making a good match requires that managers possess rich and detailed information about their employees and the available assignments. Such information is often difficult and time consuming to gather. Perhaps that's why good matches are so rarely made. In fact, one of the most common ways managers kill creativity is by not trying to obtain the information necessary to make good connections between people and jobs. Instead, something of a shotgun wedding occurs. The most eligible employee is wed to the most eligible—that is, the most urgent and open—assignment. Often, the results are predictably unsatisfactory for all involved.

FREEDOM

When it comes to granting freedom, the key to creativity is giving people autonomy concerning the means—that is, concerning process—but not necessarily the ends. People will be more creative, in other words, if you give them freedom to decide how to climb a particular mountain. You needn't let them choose which mountain to climb. In fact, clearly specified strategic goals often enhance people's creativity.

I'm not making the case that managers should leave their subordinates entirely out of goal- or agenda-setting discussions. But they should understand that inclusion in those discussions will not necessarily enhance creative output and certainly will not be sufficient to do so. It is far more important that whoever sets the goals also makes them clear to the organization and that these goals remain stable for a meaningful period of time. It is difficult, if not impossible, to work creatively toward a target if it keeps moving.

Autonomy around process fosters creativity because giving people freedom in how they approach their work heightens their intrinsic motivation and sense of ownership. Freedom about process also allows people to approach problems in ways that make the most of their expertise and their creative-thinking skills. The task may end up being a stretch for them, but they can use their strengths to meet the challenge.

How do executives mismanage freedom? There are two common ways. First, managers tend to change goals frequently or fail to define them clearly. Employees may have freedom around process, but if they don't know where they are headed, such freedom is pointless. And second, some managers fall short on this dimension by granting autonomy in name only. They claim that employees are "empowered" to explore the maze as they search for solutions but, in fact, the process is proscribed. Employees diverge at their own risk.

RESOURCES

The two main resources that affect creativity are time and money. Managers need to allot these resources carefully. Like matching people with the right assignments, deciding how much time and money to give to a team or project is a sophisticated judgment call that can either support or kill creativity.

Consider time. Under some circumstances, time pressure can heighten creativity. Say, for instance, that a competitor is about to launch a great product at a lower price than your offering or that society faces a serious problem and desperately needs a solution—such as an AIDS vaccine. In such situations, both the time crunch and the importance of the work legitimately make people feel that they must rush. Indeed, cases like these would be apt to increase intrinsic motivation by increasing the sense of challenge.

Organizations routinely kill creativity with fake deadlines or impossibly tight ones. The former create distrust and the latter cause burnout. In either case, people feel overcontrolled and unfulfilled—which invariably damages motivation. Moreover, creativity often takes time. It can be slow going to explore new concepts, put together unique solutions, and wander through the maze. Managers who do not allow time for exploration or do not schedule in incubation periods are unwittingly standing in the way of the creative process.

When it comes to project resources, again managers must make a fit. They must determine the funding, people, and other resources that a team legitimately needs to complete an assignment—and they must know how much the organization can legitimately afford to allocate to the assignment. Then they must strike a compromise. Interestingly, adding more resources above a "threshold of sufficiency" does not boost creativity. Below that threshold, however, a restriction of resources can dampen creativity. Unfortunately, many managers don't realize this and therefore often make another mistake. They keep resources tight, which pushes people to channel their creativity into finding additional resources, not in actually developing new products or services.

Another resource that is misunderstood when it comes to creativity is physical space. It is almost conventional wisdom that creative teams need open, comfortable offices. Such an atmosphere won't hurt creativity, and it may even help, but it is not nearly as important as other managerial initiatives that influence creativity. Indeed, a problem we have seen time and time again is managers paying attention to creating the "right" physical space at the expense of more high-impact actions, such as matching people to the right assignments and granting freedom around work processes.

WORK-GROUP FEATURES

If you want to build teams that come up with creative ideas, you must pay careful attention to the design of such teams. That is, you must create mutually supportive groups with a diversity of perspectives and backgrounds. Why? Because when teams comprise people with various intellectual foundations and approaches to work—that is, different expertise and creative thinking styles—ideas often combine and combust in exciting and useful ways.

Diversity, however, is only a starting point. Managers must also make sure that the teams they put together have three other features. First, the members must share excitement over the team's goal. Second, members must display a willingness to help their teammates through difficult periods and setbacks. And third, every member must recognize the unique knowledge and perspective that other members bring to the table. These factors enhance not only intrinsic motivation but also expertise and creative-thinking skills.

Again, creating such teams requires managers to have a deep understanding of their people. They must be able to assess them not just for their knowledge but for their attitudes about potential fellow team members and the collaborative process, for their problem-solving styles, and for their motivational hot buttons. Putting together a team with just the right chemistry—just the right level of diversity and supportiveness—can be difficult, but our research shows how powerful it can be.

It follows, then, that one common way managers kill creativity is by assembling homogeneous teams. The lure to do so is great. Homogeneous teams often reach "solutions" more quickly and with less friction along the way. These teams often report high morale, too. But homogeneous teams do little to enhance expertise and creative thinking. Everyone comes to the table with a similar mind-set. They leave with the same.

SUPERVISORY ENCOURAGEMENT

Most managers are extremely busy. They are under pressure for results. It is therefore easy for them to let praise for creative efforts—not just creative successes but unsuccessful efforts, too—fall by the wayside. One very simple step managers can take to foster creativity is to not let that happen.

The connection to intrinsic motivation here is clear. Certainly, people can find their work interesting or exciting without a cheering section—for some period of time. But to *sustain* such passion, most people need to feel as if their work matters to the organization or to some important group of people. Otherwise, they might as well do their work at home and for their own personal gain.

Managers in successful, creative organizations rarely offer specific extrinsic rewards for particular outcomes. However, they freely and generously recognize creative work by individuals and teams—often before the ultimate commercial impact of those efforts is known. By contrast, managers who kill creativity do so either by failing to acknowledge innovative efforts or by greeting them with skepticism. In many companies, for instance, new ideas are met not with open minds but with time-consuming layers of evaluation—or even with harsh criticism. When someone suggests a new product or process, senior managers take weeks to respond. Or they put that person through an excruciating critique.

Not every new idea is worthy of consideration, of course, but in many organizations, managers habitually demonstrate a reaction that damages creativity. They look for reasons to not use a new idea instead of searching for reasons to explore it further. An interesting psychological dynamic underlies this phenomenon. Our research shows that people believe that they will appear smarter to their bosses if they are more critical—and it often works. In many organizations, it is professionally rewarding to react critically to new ideas.

Unfortunately, this sort of negativity bias can have severe consequences for the creativity of those being evaluated. How? First, a culture of evaluation leads people to focus on the external rewards and punishments associated with their output, thus increasing the presence of extrinsic motivation and its potentially negative effects on intrinsic motivation. Second, such a culture creates a climate of fear, which again undermines intrinsic motivation.

Finally, negativity also shows up in how managers treat people whose ideas don't pan out: often, they are terminated or otherwise warehoused within the organization. Of course, ultimately, ideas do need to work; remember that creative ideas in business must be new *and* useful. The dilemma is that you can't possibly know beforehand which ideas will pan out. Furthermore, dead ends can sometimes be very enlightening. In many business situations, knowing what doesn't work can be as useful as knowing what does. But if people do not perceive any "failure value" for projects that ultimately do not achieve commercial success, they'll become less and less likely to experiment, explore, and connect with their work on a personal level. Their intrinsic motivation will evaporate.

Supervisory encouragement comes in other forms besides rewards and punishment. Another way managers can support creativity is to serve as role models, persevering through tough problems as well as encouraging collaboration and communication within the team. Such behavior enhances all three components of the creative process, and it has the added virtue of being a high-impact practice that a single manager can take on his or her own. It is better still when all managers in an organization serve as role models for the attitudes and behaviors that encourage and nurture creativity.

ORGANIZATIONAL SUPPORT

Encouragement from supervisors certainly fosters creativity, but creativity is truly enhanced when the entire organization supports it. Such support is the job of an organization's leaders, who must put in place appropriate systems or procedures and emphasize values that make it clear that creative efforts are a top priority. For example, creativity-supporting organizations consistently reward creativity, but they avoid using money to "bribe" people to come up with innovative ideas. Because monetary rewards make people feel as if they are being controlled, such a tactic probably won't work. At the same time, not providing sufficient recognition and rewards for creativity can spawn negative feelings within an organization. People can feel used, or at the least underappreciated, for their creative efforts. And it is rare to find the energy and passion of intrinsic motivation coupled with resentment.

Most important, an organization's leaders can support creativity by mandating information sharing and collaboration and by ensuring that political problems do not fester. Information sharing and collaboration support all three components of creativity. Take expertise. The more often people exchange ideas and data by working together, the more knowledge they will have. The same dynamic can be said for creative thinking. In fact, one way to enhance the creative thinking of employees is to expose them to various approaches to problem solving. With the exception of hardened misanthropes, information sharing and collaboration heighten peoples' enjoyment of work and thus their intrinsic motivation.

Whether or not you are seeking to enhance creativity, it is probably never a good idea to let political problems fester in an organizational setting. Infighting, politicking, and gossip are particularly damaging to creativity because they take peoples' attention away from work. That sense of mutual purpose and excitement so central to intrinsic motivation invariably lessens when people are cliquish or at war with one another. Indeed, our research suggests that intrinsic motivation increases when people are aware that those around them are excited by their jobs. When political problems abound, people feel that their work is threatened by others' agendas.

Finally, politicking also undermines expertise. The reason? Politics get in the way of open communication, obstructing the flow of information from point A to point B. Knowledge stays put and expertise suffers.

From the Individual to the Organization

Can executives build entire organizations that support creativity? The answer is yes. Consider the results of an intensive research project we recently completed called the Team Events Study. Over the course of two years, we studied more than two dozen teams in seven companies across three industries: high tech, consumer products, and chemicals. By following each team every day through the entire course of a creative project, we had a window into the details of what happened as the project progressed—or failed to progress, as the case may be. We did this through daily confidential e-mail reports from every person on each of the teams. At the end of each project, and at several points along the way, we used confidential reports from company experts and from team members to assess the level of creativity used in problem solving as well as the overall success of the project.

As might be expected, the teams and the companies varied widely in how successful they were at producing creative work. One organization, which I will call Chemical Central Research, seemed to be a veritable hotbed of creativity. Chemical Central supplied its parent organization with new formulations for a wide variety of industrial and consumer products. In many respects, however, members of Chemical Central's development teams were unremarkable. They were well educated, but no more so than people in many other companies we had studied. The company was doing well financially, but not enormously better than most other companies. What seemed to distinguish this organization was the quality of leadership at both the top-management level and the team level. The way managers formed teams, communicated with them, and supported their work enabled them to establish an organization in which creativity was continually stimulated.

We saw managers making excellent matches between people and assignments again and again at Chemical Central. On occasion, team members were initially unsure of whether they were up to the challenge they were given. Almost invariably, though, they found their passion and interest growing through a deep involvement in the work. Their managers knew to match them with jobs that had them working at the top of their competency levels, pushing the frontiers of their skills, and developing new competencies. But managers were careful not to allow too big a gap between employees' assignments and their abilities.

Moreover, managers at Chemical Central collaborated with the teams from the outset of a project to clarify goals. The final goals, however, were set by the managers. Then, at the day-to-day operational level, the teams were given a great deal of autonomy to make their own decisions about product development. Throughout the project, the teams' leaders and top-level managers periodically checked to see that work was directed toward the overall goals. But people were given real freedom around the implementation of the goals.

As for work-group design, every Chemical Central team, though relatively small (between four and nine members), included members of diverse professional and ethnic backgrounds. Occasionally, that diversity led to communication difficulties. But more often, it sparked new insights and allowed the teams to come up with a wider variety of ways to accomplish their goals.

One team, for example, was responsible for devising a new way to make a major ingredient for one of the company's most important products. Because managers at Chemical Central had worked consciously to create a diverse team, it happened that one member had both a legal and a technical background. This person realized that the team might well be able to patent its core idea, giving the company a clear advantage in a new market. Because team members were mutually supportive, that member was willing and eager to work closely with the inventor. Together, these individuals helped the team navigate its way through the patent application process. The team was successful and had fun along the way.

Supervisory encouragement and organizational support were also widespread at Chemical Central. For instance, a member of one team received a company award as an outstanding scientist even though, along the way, he had experienced many failures as well as successes. At one point, after spending a great deal of time on one experiment, he told us, "All I came up with was a pot of junk." Still, the company did not punish or warehouse him because of a creative effort that had failed. Instead, he was publicly lauded for his consistently creative work.

Finally, Chemical Central's leaders did much to encourage teams to seek support from all units within their divisions and to encourage collaboration across all quarters. The general manager of the research unit himself set an example, offering both strategic and technical ideas whenever teams approached him for help. Indeed, he explicitly made cross-team support a priority among top scientists in the organization. As a result, such support was expected and recognized.

For example, one team was about to test a new formulation for one of the company's major products. Because the team was small, it had to rely on a materials-analysis group within the organization to help conduct the tests. The analysis group not only helped out but also set aside generous blocks of time during the week before testing to help the team understand the nature and limits of the information the group would provide, when they would have it, and what they would need from the team to support them effectively. Members of the team were confident that they could rely on the materials-analysis group throughout the process, and the trials went well—despite the usual technical difficulties encountered in such testing.

By contrast, consider what we observed at another company in our study, a consumer products company we'll call National Houseware Products. For years, National had been well known for its innovation. But recently, the company had been restructured to accommodate a major growth spurt, and many senior managers had been fired or transferred. National's work environment had undergone drastic changes. At the same time, new product successes and new business ideas seemed to be slowing to a trickle. Interestingly, the daily reports of the Team Events Study revealed that virtually all creativity killers were present.

Managers undermined autonomy by continually changing goals and interfering with processes. At one quarterly review meeting, for example, four priorities that had been defined by management at the previous quarterly review meeting were not even mentioned. In another instance, a product that had been identified as the team's number one project was suddenly dropped without explanation.

Resources were similarly mismanaged. For instance, management perennially put teams under severe and seemingly arbitrary time and resource constraints. At first, many team members were energized by the fire-fighting atmosphere. They threw themselves into their work and rallied. But after a few months, their verve had diminished, especially because the pressures had proved meaningless.

But perhaps National's managers damaged creativity most with their approach to evaluation. They were routinely critical of new suggestions. One employee told us that he was afraid to tell his managers about some radical ideas that he had developed to grow his area of the business. The employee was wildly enthusiastic about the potential for his ideas but ultimately didn't mention them to any of his bosses. He wondered why he should bother talking about new ideas when each one was studied for all its flaws instead of its potential. Through its actions, management had too often sent the message that any big ideas about how to change the status quo would be carefully scrutinized. Those individuals brave enough to suggest new ideas had to endure long—often nasty—meetings, replete with suspicious questions.

In another example, when a team took a new competitive pricing program to the boss, it was told that a discussion of the idea would have to wait another month. One exasperated team member noted, "We analyze so long, we've lost the business before we've taken any action at all!"

Yet another National team had put in particularly long hours over a period of several weeks to create a radically improved version of a major product. The team succeeded in bringing out the product on time and in budget, and it garnered promising market response. But management acted as if everything were business as usual, providing no recognition or reward to the team. A couple of months later, when we visited the team to report the results of our study, we learned that the team leader had just accepted a job from a smaller competitor. He confided that although he felt that the opportunities for advancement and ultimate visibility may have been greater at National, he believed his work and his ideas would be valued more highly somewhere else.

And finally, the managers at National allowed political problems to fester. Consider the time a National team came up with a great idea to save money in manufacturing a new product—which was especially urgent because a competitor had just come out with a similar product at a lower price. The plan was nixed. As a matter of "policy"—a code word for long-held allegiances and rivalries within the company—the manufacturing division wouldn't allow it. One team member commented, "If facts and figures instead of politics reigned supreme, this would be a no-brainer. There are no definable cost savings from running the products where they do, and there is no counterproposal on how to save the money another way. It's just 'No!' because this is the way they want it."

Great Rewards and Risks

The important lesson of the National and Chemical Central stories is that fostering creativity is in the hands of managers as they think about, design, and establish the work environment. Creativity often requires that managers radically change the ways in which they build and interact with work groups. In many respects, it calls for a conscious culture change. But it can be done, and the rewards can be great.

The risks of not doing so may be even greater. When creativity is killed, an organization loses a potent competitive weapon: new ideas. It can also lose the energy and commitment of its people. Indeed, in all my years of research into creativity, perhaps the most difficult part has been hearing people complain that they feel stifled, frustrated, and shut down by their organizations. As one team member at National told us, "By the time I get home every day, I feel physically, emotionally, and intellectually drained. Help!"

Even if organizations seemed trapped in organizational ecosystems that kill creativity—as in the case of National Houseware Products—it is still possible to effect widespread change. Consider a recent transformation at Procter & Gamble. Once a hotbed of creativity, P&G had in recent years seen the number of its product innovations decline significantly. In response, the company established Corporate New Ventures (CNV), a small cross-functional team that embodies many of the creativity-enhancing practices described in this article.

In terms of challenge, for instance, members of the CNV team were allowed to elect themselves. How better to make sure someone is intrinsically motivated for an assignment than to ask for volunteers? Building a team from volunteers, it should be noted, was a major departure from standard P&G procedures. Members of the CNV team also were given a clear, challenging strategic goal: to invent radical new products that would build the company's future. Again departing from typical P&G practices, the team was given enormous latitude around how, when, and where they approached their work.

The list of how CNV broke with P&G's creativity-killing practices is a long one. On nearly every creativity-support dimension in the KEYS work-environment survey, CNV scored higher than national norms and higher than the pre-CNV environment at P&G. But more important than the particulars is the question: Has the changed environment resulted in more creative work? Undeniably so, and the evidence is convincing. In the three years since its inception, CNV has handed off 11 projects to the business sectors for execution. And as of early 1998, those products were beginning to flow out of the pipeline. The first product, designed to provide portable heat for several hours' relief of minor pain, was already in test marketing. And six other products were slated to go to test market within a year. Not surprisingly, given CNV's success, P&G is beginning to expand both the size and the scope of its CNV venture.

Even if you believe that your organization fosters creativity, take a hard look for creativity killers. Some of them may be flourishing in a dark corner—or even in the light. But rooting out creativity-killing behaviors isn't enough. You have to make a conscious effort to support creativity. The result can be a truly innovative company where creativity doesn't just survive but actually thrives.

The Creativity Maze

TO UNDERSTAND THE DIFFERENCES between extrinsic and intrinsic motivation, imagine a business problem as a maze.

One person might be motivated to make it through the maze as quickly and safely as possible in order to get a tangible reward, such as money—the same way a mouse would rush through for a piece of cheese. This person would look for the simplest, most straightforward path and then take it. In fact, if he is in a real rush to get that reward, he might just take the most beaten path and solve the problem exactly as it has been solved before.

That approach, based on extrinsic motivation, will indeed get him out of the maze. But the solution that arises from the process is likely to be unimaginative. It won't provide new insights about the nature of the problem or reveal new ways of looking at it. The rote solution probably won't move the business forward.

Another person might have a different approach to the maze. She might actually find the process of wandering around the different paths—the challenge and exploration itself—fun and intriguing. No doubt, this journey will take longer and include mistakes, because any maze—any truly complex problem—has many more dead ends than exits. But when the intrinsically motivated person finally does find a way out of the maze—a solution—it very likely will be more interesting than the rote algorithm. It will be more creative.

There is abundant evidence of strong intrinsic motivation in the stories of widely recognized creative people. When asked what makes the difference between creative scientists and those who are less creative, the Nobel-prize-winning physicist Arthur Schawlow said, "The labor-of-love aspect is important. The most successful scientists often are not the most talented, but the ones who are just impelled by curiosity. They've got to know what the answer is." Albert Einstein talked about intrinsic motivation as "the enjoyment of seeing and searching." The novelist John Irving, in discussing the very long hours he put into his writing, said, "The unspoken factor is love. The reason I can work so hard at my writing is that it's not work for me." And Michael Jordan, perhaps the most creative basketball player ever, had a "love of the game" clause inserted into his contract; he insisted that he be free to play pick-up basketball games any time he wished.

Creative people are rarely superstars like Michael Jordan. Indeed, most of the creative work done in the business world today gets done by people whose names will never be recorded in history books. They are people with expertise, good creative-thinking skills, and high levels of intrinsic motivation. And just as important, they work in organizations where managers consciously build environments that support these characteristics instead of destroying them.

Suggested Readings

1. Teresa M. Amabile, *Creativity in Context: Update to the Social Psychology of Creativity* (Boulder, CO: Westview Press, 1996).

2. Teresa M. Amabile, Robert Burnside, and Stanley S. Gryskiewicz, *User's Manual for KEYS: Assessing the Climate for Creativity* (Greensboro, NC: Center for Creative Leadership, 1998).

3. Rosabeth Moss Kanter, *Frontiers of Management* (Boston, MA: Harvard Business School Press, 1997).

Originally published in September–October 1998
Reprint 98501

Speeding Up Team Learning

AMY EDMONDSON, RICHARD BOHMER, AND
GARY PISANO

Executive Summary

CARDIAC SURGERY IS ONE OF medicine's modern miracles. In an operating room no larger than many household kitchens, a patient is rendered functionally dead while a surgical team repairs or replaces damaged arteries or valves. Each operation requires incredible teamwork—a single error can have disastrous consequences. In other words, surgical teams are not all that different from the cross-functional teams that have become crucial to business success.

The challenge of team management these days is not simply to execute existing processes efficiently. It's to implement new processes—as quickly as possible. But adopting new technologies or new business processes is highly disruptive, regardless of industry. The authors studied how surgical teams at 16 major medical centers implemented a difficult new procedure for performing

137

cardiac surgery. The setting was ideal for rigorously focusing on how teams learn and why some learn faster than others.

The authors found that the most successful teams had leaders who actively managed the groups' learning efforts. Teams that most successfully implemented the new technology shared three essential characteristics. They were designed for learning; their leader framed the challenge so that team members were highly motivated to learn; and an environment of psychological safety fostered communication and innovation.

The finding that teams learn more quickly if they are explicitly managed for learning poses a challenge in many areas of business. Team leaders in business tend to be chosen more for their technical expertise than for their management skills. Team leaders need to become adept at creating learning environments, and senior managers need to look beyond technical competence and identify leaders who can motivate and manage teams of disparate specialists.

CARDIAC SURGERY IS ONE OF medicine's modern miracles. In an operating room no larger than many household kitchens, a patient is rendered functionally dead—the heart no longer beating, the lungs no longer breathing—while a surgical team repairs or replaces damaged arteries or valves. A week later, the patient walks out of the hospital.

The miracle is a testament to medical technology— but also to incredible teamwork. A cardiac surgical team includes an array of specialists who need to work in close cooperation for the operation to succeed. A single error, miscommunication, or slow response can have disastrous consequences. In other words, surgical teams are not all that different from the cross-functional teams that in recent years have become crucial to business success.

We studied how surgical teams at 16 major medical centers implemented a difficult new procedure for performing cardiac surgery. What we found sheds light on one of the key determinants of team performance: a team's ability to adapt to a new way of working. In corporate settings, teams frequently have to learn new technologies or processes that are designed to improve performance. Often, however, things get worse—sometimes for a long time—before they get better. Team members may find it hard to break out of deeply ingrained routines. Or they may struggle to adjust to new roles and communication requirements.

When a product development team adopts computer-aided design tools, for example, designers, test engineers, process engineers, and even marketers have to learn the technology. But they also have to create and become comfortable with entirely new relationships, working collaboratively instead of making contributions individually and then handing pieces of the project off to the next person.

Most teams become proficient at new tasks or processes over time. But time is a luxury few teams—or companies—have. If you move too slowly, you may find that competitors are reaping the benefits of a new technology while you're still in the learning stages or that an even newer technology has superseded the one you're finally integrating into your work. The challenge of team management these days is not simply to execute existing processes efficiently. It's to implement new processes— as quickly as possible.

Whether in a hospital or an office park, getting a team up to speed isn't easy. As a surgeon on one of the teams we studied wryly put it, the new surgical procedure represented "a transfer of pain—from the patient to the surgeon." But if that came as no surprise, we *were* surprised at some of the things that helped, or didn't help, certain teams learn faster than others. An overriding lesson was that the most successful teams had leaders who actively managed their teams' learning efforts. That finding is likely to pose a challenge in many areas of business where, as in medicine, team leaders are chosen more for their technical expertise than for their management skills.

Teamwork in Operation

A conventional cardiac operation, which typically lasts two to four hours, unites four professions and a battery of specialized equipment in a carefully choreographed routine. The surgeon and the surgeon's assistant are supported by a scrub nurse, a cardiac anesthesiologist, and a perfusionist—a technician who runs the bypass machine that takes over the functions of the heart and lungs. A team in a typical cardiac surgery department performs hundreds of open-heart operations a year. Consequently, the well-defined sequence of individual tasks that constitute an operation becomes so routine that team members often don't need words to signal the start of a new stage in the procedure; a mere look is enough.

Open-heart surgery has saved countless lives, but its invasiveness—the surgeon must cut open the patient's chest and split the breastbone—has meant a painful and lengthy recovery. Recently, however, a new technology has enabled surgical teams to perform "minimally invasive cardiac surgery" in which the surgeon works through a relatively small incision between the ribs. The procedure, introduced in hospitals in the late 1990s, held out the promise of a much shorter and more pleasant recovery for thousands of patients—and a potential competitive advantage for the hospitals that adopted it. (For a description of the procedure, see "A New Way to Mend a Broken Heart" at the end of this article.)

Although the scene and players remain the same, the new technology significantly alters the nature of the surgical team's work. Obviously, individual team members need to learn new tasks. The surgeon, with the heart no longer laid out in full view, has to operate without the visual and tactile cues that typically guide this painstaking work. The anesthesiologist has to use ultrasound imaging equipment, never before a part of cardiac operations. But the mastery of new tasks isn't the only challenge. In the new procedure, a number of familiar tasks occur in a different sequence, requiring a team to unlearn the old routine before learning the new one.

More subtly, the new technology requires greater interdependence and communication among team members. For example, much of the information about the patient's heart that the surgeon traditionally gleaned through sight and touch is now delivered via digital readouts and ultrasound images displayed on monitors out of his or her field of vision. Thus the surgeon must rely on team members for essential information, disrupting not only the team's routine but also the surgeon's role as order giver in the operating room's tightly structured hierarchy.

Isolating the "Fast Factors"

The 16 teams we studied were among those that adopted this demanding new procedure. Given its complexity, they exercised great care in carrying it out, checking and double-checking every step. As a result, the rate of deaths and serious complications was no higher than for conventional procedures. But the teams were taking too long. At every hospital we studied, operations using the new technology initially took two to three times longer than conventional open-heart procedures.

Time is important in cardiac surgery. Long operations put patients at risk and strain operating teams, both mentally and physically. And with operating-room time costly and profit margins for cardiac surgery relatively high, cash-strapped hospitals want to maximize the number of operations cardiac teams perform daily.

As teams at the various hospitals struggled with the new procedure, they did get faster. This underscored one of the key tenets of learning, that the more you do something, the better you get at it. But a striking fact emerged from our research: The pace of improvement differed dramatically from team to team. Our goal was to find out what allowed certain teams to extract disproportionate amounts of learning from each increment of experience and thereby learn more quickly than their counterparts at other hospitals.

The adoption of the new technology provided an ideal laboratory for rigorously studying how teams learn and why some learn faster than others. We collected detailed data on 660 patients who underwent minimally invasive cardiac surgery at the 16 medical centers, beginning with each team's first such operation. We also interviewed in person all staff members who were involved in adopting the technology. Then we used standard statistical methods to analyze how quickly procedure times fell with accumulated experience, adjusting for variables that might influence operating time, such as the type of operation and the patient's condition. Using these and other data, we also assessed the technology implementation effort at each hospital.

Because teams doing conventional cardiac surgery follow widely accepted protocols and use standardized technology, the teams adopting the new procedure started with a common set of practices and norms. They also received the same three-day training program in the new technology. This consistency among teams in both their traditional work practices and their preparation for the new task helped us zero in on the "fast factors" that allowed some teams to adopt the technology relatively quickly.

Rethinking Conventional Wisdom

We were surprised by some of the factors that turned out not to matter in how quickly teams learned. For instance, variations among the teams in educational background and surgical experience didn't necessarily have any impact on the steepness of the learning curve. (For a comparison of teams at two medical centers, see "A Tale of Two Hospitals" at the end of this article.)

We also turned up evidence that countered several cherished notions about the ways organizations—and, by implication, teams—adopt new technologies and processes. For one thing, high-level management support for the minimally invasive technology wasn't decisive in hospitals' success in implementing it. At some hospitals, implementation was unsuccessful despite strong vocal and financial support from senior officials. At others, teams enjoyed tremendous success despite support that was ambivalent at best. For example, one surgeon initially had difficulty convincing hospital administrators that the new procedure should be tried there; they saw it as a time-consuming distraction that might benefit surgeons but would further tax the overworked hospital staff. Even so, the surgeon's team became one of the more successful in our study.

The status of the surgeon who led the team also didn't seem to make a difference. Conventional wisdom holds that a team charged with implementing a new technology or process needs a leader who has clout within the organization—someone who can "make things happen" in support of the team's efforts. But we saw situations in which department heads and world-renowned cardiac surgeons couldn't get their teams to adapt to the new operating routine. At other sites, relatively junior surgeons championed the new technology and, with little support from more senior colleagues, brought their teams quickly along the learning curve.

Finally, the debriefs, project audits, and after-action reports so often cited as key to learning weren't pivotal to the success or failure of the teams we studied. In fact, few surgical teams had time for regular, formal reviews of their work. At one hospital, such reviews were normally conducted at midnight over take-out Chinese food. Some research-oriented academic medical centers did aggregate performance data and analyze the data retrospectively, but teams at these hospitals didn't necessarily improve at faster rates. Instead, as we will discuss, the successful teams engaged in real-time learning—analyzing and drawing lessons from the process while it was under way.

Creating a Learning Team

We found that success in learning came down to the way teams were put together and how they drew on their experiences—in other words, on the teams' design and management. Teams that learned the new procedure most quickly shared three essential characteristics. They were designed for learning; their leaders framed the challenge in such a way that team members were highly motivated to learn; and the leaders' behavior created an environment of psychological safety that fostered communication and innovation.

DESIGNING A TEAM FOR LEARNING

Team leaders often have considerable discretion in determining, through choice of members, the group's mix of skills and areas of expertise. The teams in our study had no such leeway—cardiac surgery requires a surgeon, an anesthesiologist, a perfusionist, and a scrub nurse. But the leaders who capitalized on the opportunity to choose particular individuals from those specialties reaped significant benefits.

At one extreme, the leaders—the surgeons—took little initiative in choosing team members. At one hospital, the staff members chosen for training in the procedure were, essentially, those who happened to be available the weekend of the training session.

In a few teams, however, selection was much more collaborative, and the choices were carefully weighed. An anesthesiology department head, for instance, might get significant input from the cardiac surgeon before choosing an anesthesiologist. Selection was based not only on competence but also on such factors as the individual's ability to work with others, willingness to deal with new and ambiguous situations, and confidence in offering suggestions to team members with higher status.

Another critical aspect of team design was the degree to which substitutions were permitted. In conventional surgery, all members of the surgical department are assumed to be equally capable of doing the work of their particular discipline, and team members within a discipline are readily substituted for one another. It's logical to assume that training additional team members would allow for more cases to be performed using the new procedure, but we found that such flexibility has a cost. Reductions in average procedure time (adjusted for patient complexity) were faster at hospitals that kept the original teams intact.

At one hospital where several additional members of the nursing, anesthesiology, and perfusion staff were trained in the new procedure shortly after adoption, the makeup of the team changed with almost every operation. Again and again, teams had to learn from scratch how to work together. After the tenth time, the surgeon demanded a fixed team whenever he performed the new procedure. Operations went more smoothly after that.

FRAMING THE CHALLENGE

When discussing the new procedure with team members, the leaders of teams that successfully implemented the new technology characterized adopting it as an organizational challenge rather than a technical one. They emphasized the importance of creating new ways of working together over simply acquiring new individual skills. They made it clear that this reinvention of working relationships would require the contribution of every team member.

By all accounts, the difficulty of the new procedure makes cardiac surgery even more stressful than usual, at least initially. But many surgeons didn't acknowledge the higher level of stress or help their teams internalize the rationale for taking on this significant new challenge. Instead, they portrayed the technology as a plug-in component in an otherwise unchanged procedure. As one surgeon told us: "I don't see what's really new here. All the basic components of this technology have been around for years." This view led to frustration and resistance among team members. Another surgeon, who characterized the procedure as primarily a technical challenge for surgeons, was assisted by a nurse who, with grim humor, said she would rather slit her wrists than do the new procedure one more time. Her attitude was shared by many we interviewed.

But that attitude wasn't universal. At some hospitals, staff members were excited to be "part of something new," as one expressed it. A nurse reported that she felt honored to be a member of the team, in part because it was "exciting to see patients do so well." The leaders of teams with positive attitudes toward the challenge explicitly acknowledged that the task was difficult and emphasized the importance of each person's contribution. The surgeon who talked of the transfer of pain from the patient to the surgical team helped his team by highlighting, with light humor, the frustration they all faced in this learning challenge.

CREATING AN ENVIRONMENT OF PSYCHOLOGICAL SAFETY

Teams, even more than individuals, learn through trial and error. Because of the many interactions among members, it's very difficult for teams to perform tasks smoothly the first time, despite well-designed training programs and extensive individual preparation. The fastest-learning teams in our study tried different approaches in an effort to shave time from the operation without endangering patients. Indeed, team members uniformly emphasized the importance of experimenting with new ways of doing things to improve team performance—even if some of the new ways turned out not to work.

As we have noted, this learning in action proved to be more effective than the after-action analysis so often touted as key to organizational learning. Real-time learning occasionally yielded insights that might have been lost had a team member waited for a formal review session. During a procedure at one hospital, for instance, a nurse spontaneously suggested solving a surgical problem with a long-discarded type of clamp affectionately known as the "iron intern." The use of the nearly forgotten medical device immediately became part of that team's permanent routine.

When individuals learn, the process of trial and error—propose something, try it, then accept or reject it—occurs in private. But on a team, people risk appearing ignorant or incompetent when they suggest or try something new. This is particularly true in the case of technology implementation, because new technologies often render many of the skills of current "experts" irrelevant. Neutralizing the fear of embarrassment is necessary in order to achieve the robust back-and-forth communication among team members required for real-time learning.

Teams whose members felt comfortable making suggestions, trying things that might not work, pointing out potential problems, and admitting mistakes were more successful in learning the new procedure. By contrast, when people felt uneasy acting this way, the learning process was stifled.

Although the formal training for the new procedure emphasized the need for everyone on the team to speak up with observations, concerns, and questions while using the technology, such feedback often didn't happen. One team member even reported being upbraided for pointing out what he believed to be a life-threatening situation. More typical was the comment of one nurse: "If you observe something that might be a problem, you are obligated to speak up, but you choose your time. I will work around the surgeon and go through his PA [physician's assistant] if there is a problem."

But other teams clearly did foster a sense of psychological safety. How? Through the words and actions of the surgeons who acted as team leaders—not surprising, given the explicit hierarchy of the operating room. At one hospital, the surgeon told team members that they had been selected not only because of their skills but also because of the input they could provide on the process. Another surgeon, according to one of his team members, repeatedly told the team: "I need to hear from you because I'm likely to miss things." The repetition itself was important. If they hear it only once, people tend not to hear—or believe—a message that contradicts old norms.

Leading to Learn

While our research focused on the environment of cardiac surgery, we believe our findings have implications that go well beyond the operating room. Organizations in every industry encounter challenges similar to those faced by our surgical teams. Adopting new technologies or new business processes is highly disruptive, regardless of industry. Like the surgical teams in our study, business teams that use new technology for the first time must deal with a learning curve. And the learning that takes place is not just technical. It is also organizational, with teams confronting problems similar to those encountered by the surgical teams we studied: issues of status and deeply ingrained patterns of communication and behavior.

Implementing an enterprise resource planning system, for example, involves a lot of technical work in configuring databases, setting operational parameters, and ensuring that the software runs properly on a given hardware platform. The hard part for many companies, though, is not the technical side but the fact that ERP systems completely change the dynamics—the team relationships and routines—of the organization. As our study shows, it takes time for teams to learn how decisions should be made and who should talk to whom and when. It takes even longer if people don't feel comfortable speaking up.

There's yet another parallel between business teams and surgical teams. Business teams are often led by people who have been chosen because of their technical skills or expertise in a particular area: Outstanding engineers are selected to lead product development projects, IT experts lead systems implementations, and so on. These experts often find themselves in a position similar to that of the cardiac surgeons. If their teams are to succeed, they must transform themselves from technicians into leaders who can manage teams in such a way that they become learning units.

Thus the key finding of our study—that teams learn more quickly if they are explicitly managed for learning—imposes a significant new burden on many team leaders. Besides maintaining technical expertise, they need to become adept at creating environments for learning. (See "Becoming a Learning Leader" at the end of this article.) This may require them—like surgeons who give up dictatorial authority so that they can function as partners on the operating teams—to shed some of the trappings of their traditional status.

The importance of a team leader's actions suggests that the executives responsible for choosing team leaders need to rethink their own approaches. For instance, if an executive views a team's challenge as purely technical, he or she is more likely to appoint a leader based solely on technical competence. In the worst (and not unfamiliar) case, this can lead to disaster; we've all known superstar technocrats with no interpersonal skills. Clearly, there is a danger in erring too far in the other direction. If team leaders are technically incompetent, they're not only liable to make bad decisions but they also lack the credibility needed to motivate a team. But senior managers need to look beyond technical competence and identify team leaders who can motivate and manage teams of disparate specialists so that they are able to learn the skills and routines needed to succeed.

A New Way to Mend a Broken Heart

THE CARDIAC SURGERY TECHNOLOGY we studied is a modification of conventional cardiac surgery, but it requires the surgical team to take a radical new approach to working together.

The standard cardiac operation has three major phases: opening the chest, stopping the heart, and placing the patient on a heart-lung bypass machine; repairing or replacing damaged coronary arteries or valves; and weaning the patient from bypass and closing the chest wound. The minimally invasive technology, adopted by more than 100 hospitals beginning in the late 1990s, provides an alternative way to gain access to the heart. Instead of cutting through the breastbone, the surgeon uses special equipment to work on the heart through an incision between the ribs.

The small size of the incision changes open-heart surgery in several ways. For one thing, the surgeon has to operate in a severely restricted space. For another, the tubes that connect the patient to the bypass machine must be threaded through an artery and vein in the groin instead of being inserted directly into the heart through the incision. And a tiny catheter with a deflated balloon must be threaded into the aorta, the body's main artery, and the balloon inflated to act as an internal clamp. In conventional cardiac surgery, the aorta is blocked off with external clamps inserted into the open chest.

The placement of the internal clamp is an example of the greater coordination among team members required by the new procedure. Using ultrasound, the anesthesiologist works carefully with the surgeon to monitor the path of the balloon as it is inserted, because the surgeon can't see or feel the catheter. Correct placement is crucial, and the tolerances on balloon location are extremely low. Once the balloon clamp is in position, team members, including the nurse and the perfusionist, must monitor it to be sure it stays in place.

"The pressures have to be monitored on the balloon constantly," said one nurse we interviewed. "The communication with perfusion is critical. When I read the training manual, I couldn't believe it. It was so different from standard cases."

Perhaps it isn't surprising that adoption of the procedure—by all of the teams—took longer than expected. The company that developed the technology estimated that it would take surgical teams about eight operations before they were able to perform the new procedure in the same amount of time as conventional surgery. But for even the fastest-learning teams in our study, the number was closer to 40.

A Tale of Two Hospitals

THE LEADER OF THE TEAM implementing the minimally invasive surgical procedure at Chelsea Hospital was a renowned cardiac surgeon who had significant experience with the new technology. Despite that apparent advantage, his team learned the new procedure more slowly than the teams at many other hospitals, including Mountain Medical Center, where the team leader was a relatively junior surgeon with an interest in trying new techniques. Why?

The new technology as a plug-in component

Chelsea Hospital (the names of the hospitals are pseudonyms) is an urban academic medical center that at the time of our study had just hired a new chief of cardiac surgery. He seemed an ideal choice to lead the department's adoption of the new technology, as he had used the new procedure in numerous operations at another hospital (one that was not in our sample). Administrators at Chelsea supported the surgeon's request to invest in the new technology and agreed to send a team to the supplier company's formal training program.

The surgeon, however, played no role in selecting the team, which was assembled according to seniority. He also didn't participate in the team's dry run prior to the first case. He later explained that he didn't see the technique as particularly challenging, having experimented for years with placing a balloon in the aorta. Consequently, he explained, "it was not a matter of training myself. It was a matter of training the team." Such training, though, wouldn't require a change in his style of communicating with the team, he said: "Once I get the team set up, I never look up [from the operating field]. It's they who have to make sure that everything is flowing."

Mastering the new technology proved unexpectedly difficult for all team members. After almost 50 cases at Chelsea, the surgeon said: "It doesn't seem to be getting that much better. We're a little slicker, but not as slick as I would like to be." As at other sites, team members at Chelsea reported being amazed by the extent to which the procedure imposed a need for a new style and level of communication. But they were less confident than

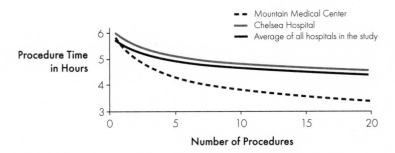

Procedure times have been adjusted for the type of operation and the severity of the patient's illness. The curves are trend lines that reflect the average improvement in procedure times.

team members at other hospitals that they would be able to put these into practice.

The new technology as a team innovation project

Mountain Medical Center is a respected community hospital serving a small city and the surrounding rural area. Although the cardiac surgery department didn't have a history of undertaking major research or cardiac surgical innovation, it had recently hired a young surgeon who took an interest in the new procedure. More than any of the team leaders at other hospitals, this surgeon recognized that implementing the technology would require the team to adopt a very different style. "The ability of the surgeon to allow himself to become a partner, not a dictator, is critical," he said. "For example, you really do have to change what you're doing [during an operation] based on a suggestion from someone else on the team. This is a complete restructuring of the [operating room] and how it works."

Team members, who were picked by the surgeon based on their experience working together, responded enthusiastically to his approach. One noted that the "hierarchy [has] changed," creating a "free and open environment with input from everybody." Said another: "I'm so excited about [the new procedure]. It has been a model, not just for this hospital but for cardiac surgery. It is about what a group of people can do." He explained that the team got better because "the surgeon said, 'Hey, you guys have got to make this thing work.' That's a great motivator."

In the end, despite the team leader's modest reputation and the hospital's limited experience in implementing new cardiac procedures, Mountain Medical was one of the two hospitals in our study that learned the new technology most quickly.

Becoming a Learning Leader

CREATING AN ENVIRONMENT conducive to team learning isn't hard, but it does require a team leader to act quickly. Social psychologists have shown that people watch their supervisors carefully for cues on how team members are expected to behave. These impressions form early in the life of a group or project. To set the right tone, team leaders must:

Be accessible

In order to make clear that others' opinions are welcomed and valued, the leader must be available, not aloof. One nurse in our study commented about a successful team leader: "He's in his office, always just two seconds away. He can always take five minutes to explain something, and he never makes you feel stupid."

Ask for input

An atmosphere of information sharing can be reinforced by an explicit request from the team leader for contributions from members. The surgeon on one successful team "told us to immediately let him know—let everyone know—if anything is out of place," said the team's perfusionist.

Serve as a "fallibility model"

Team leaders can further foster a learning environment by admitting their mistakes to the team. One surgeon in our study explicitly acknowledged his shortcomings.

"He'll say, 'I screwed up. My judgment was bad in that case,'" a team member reported. That signaled to others on the team that errors and concerns could be discussed without fear of punishment.

Originally published in October 2001
Reprint R0109J

What You Don't Know About Making Decisions

DAVID A. GARVIN AND

MICHAEL A. ROBERTO

Executive Summary

MOST EXECUTIVES THINK OF decision making as a
singular event that occurs at a particular point in time. In
reality, though, decision making is a process fraught with
power plays, politics fraught with power plays, politics,
personal nuances, and institutional history. Leaders who
recognize this make far better decisions than those who
persevere in the fantasy that decisions are events they
alone control.

That said, some decision-making processes are far
more effective than others. Most often, participants use an
advocacy process, possibly the least productive way to
get things done. They view decision making as a contest,
arguing passionately for their preferred solutions, present-
ing information selectively, withholding relevant conflicting
data so they can make a convincing case, and standing
firm against opposition. Much more powerful is an *inquiry*

159

process, in which people consider a variety of options and work together to discover the best solution. Moving from advocacy to inquiry requires careful attention to three critical factors: fostering constructive, rather than personal, conflict; making sure everyone knows that their viewpoints are given serious consideration even if they are not ultimately accepted; and knowing when to bring deliberations to a close.

The authors discuss in detail strategies for moving from an advocacy to an inquiry process, as well as for fostering productive conflict, true consideration, and timely closure. And they offer a framework for assessing the effectiveness of your process while you're still in the middle of it.

Decision making is a job that lies at the very heart of leadership and one that requires a genius for balance: the ability to embrace the divergence that may characterize early discussions and to forge the unity needed for effective implementation.

LEADERS SHOW THEIR METTLE in many ways—setting strategy and motivating people, just to mention two—but above all else leaders are made or broken by the quality of their decisions. That's a given, right? If you answered yes, then you would probably be surprised by how many executives approach decision making in a way that neither puts enough options on the table nor permits sufficient evaluation to ensure that they can make the best choice. Indeed, our research over the past several years strongly suggests that, simply put, most leaders get decision making all wrong.

The reason: Most businesspeople treat decision making as an event—a discrete choice that takes place at a single point in time, whether they're sitting at a desk, moderating a meeting, or staring at a spreadsheet. This classic view of decision making has a pronouncement popping out of a leader's head, based on experience, gut, research, or all three. Say the matter at hand is whether to pull a product with weak sales off the market. An "event" leader would mull in solitude, ask for advice, read reports, mull some more, then say yea or nay and send the organization off to make it happen. But to look at decision making that way is to overlook larger social and organizational contexts, which ultimately determine the success of any decision.

The fact is, decision making is not an event. It's a process, one that unfolds over weeks, months, or even years; one that's fraught with power plays and politics and is replete with personal nuances and institutional history; one that's rife with discussion and debate; and one that requires support at all levels of the organization when it comes time for execution. Our research shows that the difference between leaders who make good decisions and those who make bad ones is striking. The former recognize that all decisions are processes, and they explicitly design and manage them as such. The latter persevere in the fantasy that decisions are events they alone control.

In the following pages, we'll explore how leaders can design and manage a sound, effective decision-making process—an approach we call inquiry—and outline a set of criteria for assessing the quality of the decision-making process. First, a look at the process itself.

Decisions as Process: Inquiry Versus Advocacy

Not all decision-making processes are equally effective, particularly in the degree to which they allow a group to identify and consider a wide range of ideas. In our research, we've seen two broad approaches. *Inquiry*, which we prefer, is a very open process designed to generate multiple alternatives, foster the exchange of ideas, and produce a well-tested solution. Unfortunately, this approach doesn't come easily or naturally to most people. Instead, groups charged with making a decision tend to default to the second mode, one we call *advocacy*. The two look deceptively similar on the surface: groups of people, immersed in discussion and debate, trying to select a course of action by drawing on what they believe is the best available evidence. But despite their similarities, inquiry and advocacy produce dramatically different results. (See "Advocacy Versus Inquiry in Action" for a real-life example of these two approaches.)

When a group takes an advocacy perspective, participants approach decision making as a contest, although they don't necessarily compete openly or even consciously. Well-defined groups with special interests—dueling divisions in search of budget increases, for example—advocate for particular positions. Participants are passionate about their preferred solutions and therefore stand firm in the face of disagreement. That level of passion makes it nearly impossible to remain objective, limiting people's ability to pay attention to opposing arguments. Advocates often present information selectively, buttressing their arguments while withholding relevant conflicting data. Their goal, after all, is to make a compelling case, not to convey an evenhanded or balanced view. Two different plant managers pushing their own improvement programs, for example, may be wary of reporting potential weak points for fear that full disclosure will jeopardize their chances of winning the debate and gaining access to needed resources.

What's more, the disagreements that arise are frequently fractious and even antagonistic. Personalities
and egos come into play, and differences are normally
resolved through battles of wills and behind-the-scenes
maneuvering. The implicit assumption is that a superior
solution will emerge from a test of strength among competing positions. But in fact this approach typically suppresses innovation and encourages participants to go
along with the dominant view to avoid further conflict.

By contrast, an inquiry-focused group carefully con-
siders a variety of options and works together to discover
the best solution. While people naturally continue to
have their own interests, the goal is not to persuade the
group to adopt a given point of view but instead to come
to agreement on the best course of action. People share
information widely, preferably in raw form, to allow participants to draw their own conclusions. Rather than
suppressing dissension, an inquiry process encourages
critical thinking. All participants feel comfortable raising
alternative solutions and asking hard questions about
the possibilities already on the table.

People engaged in an inquiry process rigorously question proposals and the assumptions they rest on, so conflict may be intense—but it is seldom personal. In fact,
because disagreements revolve around ideas and inter-
pretations rather than entrenched positions, conflict is
generally healthy, and team members resolve their differences by applying rules of reason. The implicit assumption is that a consummate solution will emerge from a
test of strength among competing ideas rather than
dueling positions. Recent accounts of GE's succession
process describe board members pursuing just such an
open-minded approach. All members met repeatedly
with the major candidates and gathered regularly to

review their strengths and weaknesses—frequently without Jack Welch in attendance—with little or no attempt to lobby early for a particular choice.

A process characterized by inquiry rather than advocacy tends to produce decisions of higher quality—decisions that not only advance the company's objectives but also are reached in a timely manner and can be implemented effectively. Therefore, we believe that leaders seeking to improve their organizations' decision-making capabilities need to begin with a single goal: moving as quickly as possible from a process of advocacy to one of inquiry. That requires careful attention to three critical factors, the "three C's" of effective decision making: *conflict, consideration,* and *closure.* Each entails a delicate balancing act. (See the exhibit "Two Approaches to Decision Making" for more information.)

Two Approaches to Decision Making

	Advocacy	Inquiry
Concept of decision making	a contest	collaborative problem solving
Purpose of discussion	persuasion and lobbying	testing and evaluation
Participants' role	spokespeople	critical thinkers
Patterns of behavior	strive to persuade others	present balanced arguments
	defend your position	remain open to alternatives
	downplay weaknesses	accept constructive criticism
Minority views	discouraged or dismissed	cultivated and valued
Outcome	winners and losers	collective ownership

Constructive Conflict

Critical thinking and rigorous debate invariably lead to conflict. The good news is that conflict brings issues into focus, allowing leaders to make more informed choices. The bad news is that the wrong kind of conflict can derail the decision-making process altogether.

Indeed, conflict comes in two forms—*cognitive* and *affective*. Cognitive, or substantive, conflict relates to the work at hand. It involves disagreements over ideas and assumptions and differing views on the best way to proceed. Not only is such conflict healthy, it's crucial to effective inquiry. When people express differences openly and challenge underlying assumptions, they can flag real weaknesses and introduce new ideas. Affective, or interpersonal, conflict is emotional. It involves personal friction, rivalries, and clashing personalities, and it tends to diminish people's willingness to cooperate during implementation, rendering the decision-making process less effective. Not surprisingly, it is a common feature of advocacy processes.

On examination, the two are easy to distinguish. When a team member recalls "tough debates about the strategic, financial, and operating merits of the three acquisition candidates," she is referring to cognitive conflict. When a team member comments on "heated arguments that degenerated into personal attacks," he means affective conflict. But in practice the two types of conflict are surprisingly hard to separate. People tend to take any criticism personally and react defensively. The atmosphere quickly becomes charged, and even if a high-quality decision emerges, the emotional fallout tends to linger, making it hard for team members to work together during implementation.

The challenge for leaders is to increase cognitive conflict while keeping affective conflict low—no mean feat. One technique is to establish norms that make vigorous debate the rule rather than the exception. Chuck Knight, for 27 years the CEO of Emerson Electric, accomplished this by relentlessly grilling managers during planning reviews, no matter what he actually thought of the proposal on the table, asking tough, combative questions and expecting well-framed responses. The process—which Knight called the "logic of illogic" because of his willingness to test even well-crafted arguments by raising unexpected, and occasionally fanciful, concerns—was undoubtedly intimidating. But during his tenure it produced a steady stream of smart investment decisions and an unbroken string of quarterly increases in net income.

Bob Galvin, when he was CEO of Motorola in the 1980s, took a slightly different approach. He habitually asked unexpected hypothetical questions that stimulated creative thinking. Subsequently, as chairman of the board of overseers for the Malcolm Baldrige National Quality Program, Galvin took his colleagues by surprise when, in response to pressure from constituents to broaden the criteria for the award, he proposed narrowing them instead. In the end, the board did in fact broaden the criteria, but his seemingly out-of-the-blue suggestion sparked a creative and highly productive debate.

Another technique is to structure the conversation so that the process, by its very nature, fosters debate. This can be done by dividing people into groups with different, and often competing, responsibilities. For example, one group may be asked to develop a proposal while the other generates alternative recommendations. Then the groups would exchange proposals and discuss the various options. Such techniques virtually guarantee high levels of cognitive conflict. (The exhibit "Structuring the Debate" outlines two approaches for using different groups to stimulate creative thinking.)

But even if you've structured the process with an eye toward encouraging cognitive conflict, there's always a risk that it will become personal. Beyond cooling the debate with "time-outs," skilled leaders use a number of creative techniques to elevate cognitive debate while minimizing affective conflict.

First, adroit leaders pay careful attention to the way issues are framed, as well as to the language used during discussions. They preface contradictory remarks or questions with phrases that remove some of the personal sting ("Your arguments make good sense, but let me play devil's advocate for a moment"). They also set ground rules about language, insisting that team members avoid words and behavior that trigger defensiveness. For instance, in the U.S. Army's after-action reviews, conducted immediately after missions to identify mistakes so they can be avoided next time, facilitators make a point of saying, "We don't use the 'b' word, and we don't use the 'f' word. We don't place blame, and we don't find fault."

Second, leaders can help people step back from their preestablished positions by breaking up natural coalitions and assigning people to tasks on some basis other than traditional loyalties. At a leading aerospace company, one business unit president had to deal with two powerful coalitions within his organization during a critical decision about entering into a strategic alliance. When he set up two groups to consider alternative alliance partners, he interspersed the groups with

Structuring the Debate

By breaking a decision-making body into two subgroups, leaders can often create an environment in which people feel more comfortable engaging in debate. Scholars recommend two techniques in particular, which we call the "point-counterpoint" and "intellectual watchdog" approaches. The first three steps are the same for both techniques:

Point-Counterpoint	Intellectual Watchdog
The team divides into two subgroups.	The team divides into two subgroups.
Subgroup A develops a proposal, fleshing out the recommendation, the key assumptions, and the critical supporting data.	Subgroup A develops a proposal, fleshing out the recommendation, the key assumptions, and the critical supporting data.
Subgroup A presents the proposal to Subgroup B in written and oral forms.	Subgroup A presents the proposal to Subgroup B in written and oral forms.
Subgroup B generates one or more alternative plans of action.	Subgroup B develops a detailed critique of these assumptions and recommendations. It presents this critique in written and oral forms. Subgroup A revises its proposal based on this feedback.
The subgroups come together to debate the proposals and seek agreement on a common set of assumptions.	The subgroups continue in this revision-critique-revision cycle until they converge on a common set of assumptions.
Based on those assumptions, the subgroups continue to debate various options and strive to agree on a common set of recommendations.	Then, the subgroups work together to develop a common set of recommendations.

members of each coalition, forcing people with different interests to work with one another. He then asked both groups to evaluate the same wide range of options using different criteria (such as technological capability, manufacturing prowess, or project management skills). The two groups then shared their evaluations and worked together to select the best partner. Because nobody had complete information, they were forced to listen closely to one another.

Third, leaders can shift individuals out of well-grooved patterns, where vested interests are highest. They can, for example, ask team members to research and argue for a position they did not endorse during initial discussions. Similarly, they can assign team members to play functional or managerial roles different from their own, such as asking an operations executive to take the marketing view or asking a lower-level employee to assume the CEO's strategic perspective.

Finally, leaders can ask participants locked in debate to revisit key facts and assumptions and gather more information. Often, people become so focused on the differences between opposing positions that they reach a stalemate. Emotional conflict soon follows. Asking people to examine underlying presumptions can defuse the tension and set the team back on track. For instance, at Enron, when people disagree strongly about whether or not to apply their trading skills to a new commodity or market, senior executives quickly refocus the discussion on characteristics of industry structure and assumptions about market size and customer preferences. People quickly recognize areas of agreement, discover precisely how and why they disagree, and then focus their debate on specific issues.

Consideration

Once a decision's been made and the alternatives dismissed, some people will have to surrender the solution they preferred. At times, those who are overruled resist the outcome; at other times, they display grudging acceptance. What accounts for the difference? The critical factor appears to be the perception of fairness—what scholars call "procedural justice." The reality is that the leader will make the ultimate decision, but the people participating in the process must believe that their views were considered and that they had a genuine opportunity to influence the final decision. Researchers have found that if participants believe the process was fair, they are far more willing to commit themselves to the resulting decision even if their views did not prevail.

Many managers equate fairness with *voice*—with giving everyone a chance to express his or her own views. They doggedly work their way around the table, getting everyone's input. However, voice is not nearly as important as *consideration*—people's belief that the leader actively listened to them during the discussions and weighed their views carefully before reaching a decision. In his 1999 book, *Only the Paranoid Survive*, Intel's chairman Andy Grove describes how he explains the distinction to his middle managers: "Your criterion for involvement should be that you're heard and understood. . . . All sides cannot prevail in the debate, but all opinions have value in shaping the right answer."

In fact, voice without consideration is often damaging; it leads to resentment and frustration rather than to acceptance. When the time comes to implement the decision, people are likely to drag their feet if they sense that the decision-making process had been a sham—an

exercise in going through the motions designed to vali-
date the leader's preferred solution. This appears to have
been true of the Daimler-Chrysler merger. Daimler CEO
Jurgen Schrempp asked for extensive analysis and assessment of potential merger candidates but had long before
settled on Chrysler as his choice. In fact, when consultants told him that his strategy was unlikely to create
shareholder value, he dismissed the data and went ahead
with his plans. Schrempp may have solicited views from
many parties, but he clearly failed to give them much
weight.

Leaders can demonstrate consideration throughout
the decision-making process. At the outset, they need to
convey openness to new ideas and a willingness to
accept views that differ from their own. In particular,
they must avoid suggesting that their minds are already
made up. They should avoid disclosing their personal
preferences early in the process, or they should clearly
state that any initial opinions are provisional and subject
to change. Or they can absent themselves from early
deliberations.

During the discussions, leaders must take care to
show that they are listening actively and attentively.
How? By asking questions, probing for deeper explana-
tions, echoing comments, making eye contact, and showing patience when participants explain their positions.
Taking notes is an especially powerful signal, since it
suggests that the leader is making a real effort to capture, understand, and evaluate people's thoughts.

And after they make the final choice, leaders should
explain their logic. They must describe the rationale for
their decision, detailing the criteria they used to select a
course of action. Perhaps more important, they need to
convey how each participant's arguments affected the

final decision or explain clearly why they chose to differ with those views.

Closure

Knowing when to end deliberations is tricky; all too often decision-making bodies rush to a conclusion or else dither endlessly and decide too late. Deciding too early is as damaging as deciding too late, and both problems can usually be traced to unchecked advocacy.

DECIDING TOO EARLY

Sometimes people's desire to be considered team players overrides their willingness to engage in critical thinking and thoughtful analysis, so the group readily accepts the first remotely plausible option. Popularly known as "groupthink," this mind-set is prevalent in the presence of strong advocates, especially in new teams, whose members are still learning the rules and may be less willing to stand out as dissenters.

The danger of groupthink is not only that it suppresses the full range of options but also that unstated objections will come to the surface at some critical moment—usually at a time when aligned, cooperative action is essential to implementation. The leader of a large division of a fast-growing retailer learned this the hard way. He liked to work with a small subset of his senior team to generate options, evaluate the alternatives, and develop a plan of action, and then bring the proposal back to the full team for validation. At that point, his managers would feel they had been presented with a fait accompli and so would be reluctant to raise their concerns. As one of them put it: "Because the meeting is the wrong place to object, we don't walk out of the room as a unified group." Instead, they would reopen the debate during implementation, delaying important initiatives by many months.

As their first line of defense against groupthink, leaders need to learn to recognize latent discontent, paying special attention to body language: furrowed brows, crossed arms, or curled-up defiance. To bring disaffected people back into the discussion, it may be best to call for a break, approach dissenters one by one, encourage them to speak up, and then reconvene. GM's Alfred Sloan was famous for this approach, which he would introduce with the following speech: "I take it we are all in complete agreement on the decision here. Then I propose we postpone further discussion of the matter until our next meeting to give ourselves time to develop disagreement and perhaps gain some understanding of what the decision is all about."

Another way to avoid early closure is to cultivate minority views either through norms or through explicit rules. Minority views broaden and deepen debate; they stretch a group's thinking, even though they are seldom adopted intact. It is for this reason that Andy Grove routinely seeks input from "helpful Cassandras," people who are known for raising hard questions and offering fresh perspectives about the dangers of proposed policies.

DECIDING TOO LATE

Here, too, unchecked advocacy is frequently the source of the problem, and in these instances it takes two main forms. At times, a team hits gridlock: Warring factions refuse to yield, restating their positions over and over again. Without a mechanism for breaking the deadlock, discussions become an endless loop. At other times, people bend over backward to ensure evenhanded participation. Striving for fairness, team members insist on hearing every view and resolving every question before reaching a conclusion. This demand for certainty—for complete arguments backed by unassailable data—is its own peculiar form of advocacy. Once again, the result is usually an endless loop, replaying the same alternatives, objections, and requests for further information. Any member of the group can unilaterally derail the discussion by voicing doubts. Meanwhile, competitive pressures may be demanding an immediate response, or participants may have tuned out long ago, as the same arguments are repeated ad nauseam.

At this point, it's the leader's job to "call the question." Jamie Houghton, the longtime CEO of Corning, invented a vivid metaphor to describe this role. He spoke of wearing two hats when working with his senior team: He figuratively put on his cowboy hat when he wanted to debate with members as an equal, and he donned a bowler when, as CEO, he called the question and announced a decision. The former role allowed for challenges and continued discussion; the latter signaled an end to the debate.

The message here is that leaders—and their teams—need to become more comfortable with ambiguity and be willing to make speedy decisions in the absence of complete, unequivocal data or support. As Dean Stanley Teele of Harvard Business School was fond of telling students: "The art of management is the art of making meaningful generalizations out of inadequate facts."

A Litmus Test

Unfortunately, superior decision making is distressingly difficult to assess in real time. Successful outcomes—

decisions of high quality, made in a timely manner and implemented effectively—can be evaluated only after the fact. But by the time the results are in, it's normally too late to take corrective action. Is there any way to find out earlier whether you're on the right track?

There is indeed. The trick, we believe, is to periodically assess the decision-making process, even as it is under way. Scholars now have considerable evidence showing that a small set of process traits is closely linked with superior outcomes. While they are no guarantee of success, their combined presence sharply improves the odds that you'll make a good decision.

MULTIPLE ALTERNATIVES

When groups consider many alternatives, they engage in more thoughtful analysis and usually avoid settling too quickly on the easy, obvious answer. This is one reason techniques like point-counterpoint, which requires groups to generate at least two alternatives, are so often associated with superior decision making. Usually, keeping track of the number of options being considered will tell if this test has been met. But take care not to double count. Go-no-go choices involve only one option and don't qualify as two alternatives.

ASSUMPTION TESTING

"Facts" come in two varieties: those that have been carefully tested and those that have been merely asserted or assumed. Effective decision-making groups do not confuse the two. They periodically step back from their arguments and try to confirm their assumptions by examining them critically. If they find that some still lack hard evidence, they may elect to proceed, but they will at least know they're venturing into uncertain territory. Alternatively, the group may designate "intellectual watchdogs" who are assigned the task of scrutinizing the process for unchecked assumptions and challenging them on the spot.

WELL-DEFINED CRITERIA

Without crisp, clear goals, it's easy to fall into the trap of comparing apples with oranges. Competing arguments become difficult to judge, since advocates will suggest using those measures (net income, return on capital, market presence, share of mind, and so on) that favor their preferred alternative. Fuzzy thinking and long delays are the likely result.

To avoid the problem, the team should specify goals up front and revisit them repeatedly during the decision-making process. These goals can be complex and multifaceted, quantitative and qualitative, but whatever form they take, they must remain at the fore. Studies of merger decisions have found that as the process reaches its final stages and managers feel the pressure of deadlines and the rush to close, they often compromise or adjust the criteria they originally created for judging the appropriateness of the deal.

DISSENT AND DEBATE

David Hume, the great Scottish philosopher, argued persuasively for the merits of debate when he observed that the "truth springs from arguments amongst friends." There are two ways to measure the health of a debate: the kinds of questions being asked and the level of listening.

Some questions open up discussion; others narrow it and end deliberations. Contrarian hypothetical questions usually trigger healthy debate. A manager who worked for former American Express CEO Harvey Golub points to a time when the company was committed to lowering credit card fees, and Golub unexpectedly proposed raising fees instead. "I don't think he meant it seriously," says the manager. "But he certainly taught us how to think about fees."

The level of listening is an equally important indicator of a healthy decision-making process. Poor listening produces flawed analysis as well as personal friction. If participants routinely interrupt one another or pile on rebuttals before digesting the preceding comment, affective conflict is likely to materialize. Civilized discussions quickly become impossible, for collegiality and group harmony usually disappear in the absence of active listening.

PERCEIVED FAIRNESS

A real-time measure of perceived fairness is the level of participation that's maintained after a key midpoint or milestone has been reached. Often, a drop in participation is an early warning of problems with implementation since some members of the group are already showing their displeasure by voting with their feet.

In fact, keeping people involved in the process is, in the end, perhaps the most crucial factor in making a decision—and making it stick. It's a job that lies at the heart of leadership and one that uniquely combines the leader's numerous talents. It requires the fortitude to promote conflict while accepting ambiguity, the wisdom to know when to bring conversations to a close, the patience to help others understand the reasoning behind your choice, and, not least, a genius for balance— the ability to embrace both the divergence that may characterize early discussions and the unity needed for effective implementation. Cyrus the Great, the founder of the Persian Empire and a renowned military leader, understood the true hallmark of leadership in the sixth century BC, when he attributed his success to "diversity in counsel, unity in command."

Advocacy Versus Inquiry in Action: The Bay of Pigs and the Cuban Missile Crisis

PERHAPS THE BEST DEMONSTRATION of advocacy versus inquiry comes from the administration of President John F. Kennedy. During his first two years in office, Kennedy wrestled with two critical foreign policy decisions: the Bay of Pigs invasion and the Cuban Missile Crisis. Both were assigned to cabinet-level task forces, involving many of the same players, the same political interests, and extremely high stakes. But the results were extraordinarily different, largely because the two groups operated in different modes.

The first group, charged with deciding whether to support an invasion of Cuba by a small army of U.S.-trained Cuban exiles, worked in advocacy mode, and the outcome is widely regarded as an example of flawed decision making. Shortly after taking office, President Kennedy learned of the planned attack on Cuba developed by the CIA during the Eisenhower administration. Backed by the Joint Chiefs of Staff, the CIA argued forcefully for the invasion and minimized the risks, filtering the information presented to the president to reinforce the agency's position. Knowledgeable individuals on the

State Department's Latin America desk were excluded from deliberations because of their likely opposition.

Some members of Kennedy's staff opposed the plan but held their tongues for fear of appearing weak in the face of strong advocacy by the CIA. As a result, there was little debate, and the group failed to test some critical underlying assumptions. For example, they didn't question whether the landing would in fact lead to a rapid domestic uprising against Castro, and they failed to find out whether the exiles could fade into the mountains (which were 80 miles from the landing site) should they meet with strong resistance. The resulting invasion is generally considered to be one of the low points of the Cold War. About 100 lives were lost, and the rest of the exiles were taken hostage. The incident was a major embarrassment to the Kennedy administration and dealt a blow to America's global standing.

After the botched invasion, Kennedy conducted a review of the foreign policy decision-making process and introduced five major changes, essentially transforming the process into one of inquiry. First, people were urged to participate in discussions as "skeptical generalists"—that is, as disinterested critical thinkers rather than as representatives of particular departments. Second, Robert Kennedy and Theodore Sorensen were assigned the role of intellectual watchdog, expected to pursue every possible point of contention, uncovering weaknesses and untested assumptions. Third, task forces were urged to abandon the rules of protocol, eliminating formal agendas and deference to rank. Fourth, participants were expected to split occasionally into subgroups to develop a broad range of options. And finally, President Kennedy decided to absent himself from some of the early task force meetings to avoid influencing other participants and slanting the debate.

The inquiry mode was used to great effect when in October 1962 President Kennedy learned that the Soviet Union had placed nuclear missiles on Cuban soil, despite repeated assurances from the Soviet ambassador that this would not occur. Kennedy immediately convened a high-level task force, which contained many of the same men responsible for the Bay of Pigs invasion, and asked them to frame a response. The group met night and day for two weeks, often inviting additional members to join in their deliberations to broaden their perspective. Occasionally, to encourage the free flow of ideas, they met without the president. Robert Kennedy played his new role thoughtfully, critiquing options frequently and encouraging the group to develop additional alternatives. In particular, he urged the group to move beyond a simple go-no-go decision on a military air strike.

Ultimately, subgroups developed two positions, one favoring a blockade and the other an air strike. These groups gathered information from a broad range of sources, viewed and interpreted the same intelligence photos, and took great care to identify and test underlying assumptions, such as whether the Tactical Air Command was indeed capable of eliminating all Soviet missiles in a surgical air strike. The subgroups exchanged position papers, critiqued each other's proposals, and came together to debate the alternatives. They presented Kennedy with both options, leaving him to make the final choice. The result was a carefully framed response, leading to a successful blockade and a peaceful end to the crisis.

Originally published in September 2001
Reprint R0108G

About the Contributors

TERESA M. AMABILE is the M.B.A. Class of 1954 Professor of Business Administration and Senior Associate Dean for Research at Harvard Business School in Boston.

RONALD N. ASHKENAS is a Managing Partner of Robert H. Schaffer & Associates, a management consulting firm based in Stamford, Connecticut. He has written three previous articles for HBR, most recently "Integration Managers: Special Leaders for Special Times" (with Suzanne C. Francis, November–December 2000).

RICHARD BOHMER, a physician, is an Assistant Professor at Harvard Business School in Boston.

DAVID DAVIS is a Senior Executive with Tate & Lyle PLC, the U.K. sugar and trading company, where he specializes in turnarounds and problem companies. He has written articles for a variety of British and North American publications on such topics as politics, industrial relations, general management, and computers.

AMY EDMONDSON is an Associate Professor at Harvard Business School in Boston.

DAVID A. GARVIN is the Robert and Jane Cizik Professor of Business Administration at Harvard Business School in

Boston. His most recent HBR article is "Leveraging Processes for Strategic Advantage" (September–October 1995).

CHARLES H. HOUSE is the General Manager of the Software Engineering Systems Division of Hewlett-Packard in Palo Alto. Prior to this, he was HP's Corporate Engineering Director.

NADIM F. MATTA is the Senior Partner of Robert H. Schaffer & Associates, a management consulting firm based in Stamford, Connecticut. Prior to joining RHS&A, he worked for the U.S. Agency of International Development and headed the food distribution program for Save the Children during the civil war in Lebanon.

GARY PISANO is the Harry E. Figgie, Jr. Professor of Business Administration at the Harvard Business School in Boston.

RAYMOND L. PRICE is the Director of Employee Training and Development for the Boeing Commercial Airplane Group in Seattle. Previously, he was Hewlett-Packard's Manager of Engineering Education.

MICHAEL A. ROBERTO is an Assistant Professor at Harvard Business School in Boston.

JERRY ROSS is Associate Professor of Organizational Behavior at the Graduate School of Industrial Administration at Carnegie Mellon University in Pittsburgh, Pennsylvania.

ISABELLE ROYER is an Assistant Professor at the University of Paris, Dauphine, and is affiliated with the university's DMSP Research Center, which focuses on marketing and strategy issues.

BARRY M. STAW is the Mitchell Professor of Leadership and Communication at the Haas School of Business at the University of California in Berkeley. He is also Chairman of the school's Organizational Behavior and Industrial Relations Group.

Index